D0397921

THEATRE ROYAL

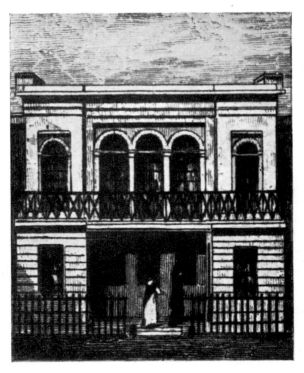

Plate I
THE FIRST BUILDING
1774

THEATRE ROYAL

*The History of the Theatre Royal
Birmingham*

by

JOHN E. CUNNINGHAM, M.A.

GEORGE RONALD
2, Alfred Street
Oxford

ALL RIGHTS RESERVED
1950

PRINTED IN ENGLAND
BY
THE TEMPLAR PRINTING WORKS
BIRMINGHAM, 3

PREFACE

THE main sources of the information in the following pages are three : a collection of playbills for the Theatre Royal, beginning in 1790; the Theatre Royal Library, consisting of about 2,000 printed and 250 manuscript plays and pantomimes, collected chiefly by Mercer Simpson, and afterwards in the possession of the late R. Crompton Rhodes ; and some 2,000 documents, legal, personal and business, which belonged to the Committee of Proprietors which was disbanded in 1900. All these materials are in Birmingham Reference Library. The play bills are in chronological order, but the other material is uncatalogued.

The Theatre Royal Library contains some very interesting prompt copies ; and the documents include the Minute Books of the Proprietors, from the very beginning. These latter have never been touched. Mr. Rhodes, when writing his *Short History of the Theatre Royal*, may have obtained material from the plays in his possession. His book, and the memoir *Ye Old Theatre Royal*, by T. E. Pemberton, although both are brief, lacking in detail, and sometimes inaccurate, have naturally been of great service in the construction of this more detailed investigation.

All pictures reproduced in the following pages are from originals in the Birmingham Reference Library.

CONTENTS

CHAPTER I

THE EARLY THEATRICAL HISTORY OF BIRMINGHAM

ALTHOUGH there is no definite evidence that liturgical drama was performed in medieval Birmingham, there is much to suggest it. The mother church of the town is Saint Martin's ; and this foundation is of great antiquity. During the rebuilding which went on in 1562, walls were unearthed which indicate a pre-Conquest structure and it is said to have dated from the eighth century. In 1382 was formed the Guild of the Holy Cross, consisting of two chantry priests in the church. This Guild developed into a large organisation, with a hall of its own, and it may well have presented religious plays. Birmingham certainly knew something of sacred pageantry, perhaps of morality and miracle plays. What is now called Carr's Lane was formerly known as God's Cart Lane, because the Holy Cart, used, it is supposed, in religious pageants, was kept there. This cart may have been the one on which relics were drawn through the streets in procession, or it may have been a triple-tiered waggon on which plays were performed. There was certainly some form of public display, if not on the scale of that in the neighbouring town of Coventry.

Two Wakes were established in the districts of Deritend and Handsworth, during the fifteenth century, and here the inhabitants may well have been initiated into the mysteries of booth drama. Our earliest account of the town's theatrical life says that it began with strolling players.

Birmingham has, however, always been an industrious place. There is testimony of its business as early as the writings of Camden, who describes it as "full of inhabitants, and resounding with hammers and anvils, for the most part of them are smiths." In such a place one might not expect to hear of very elaborate means of amusement. Some of the popular modes of entertainment are interesting. Singing, skittling, cock-fighting and bull-baiting were in regular use ; the last bull to be baited in Birmingham was in 1820. Astleys were giving equestrian displays in the fields in the last decade of the eighteenth century.

There was one local custom so odd as to be worth mention. It was called Bull-running. A bull was provided by the butchers of the town, and an announcement was made. Streets were cleared, shutters put up, and everyone was armed with a staff, on which there was to be no iron. The animal was released, and belaboured up and down the streets, until everyone had used up his energy— after which the beast was slaughtered for meat.

This busy, and rather brutal community increased rapidly after the Restoration. At that time it had about 5,500 inhabitants ; by 1700 there were 15,030.

It was at about this time that regular, seasonal performances were first given. The early players gave their entertainments in two rough sheds, which they themselves erected. One was in the Hinkleys—fields a little to the south of New Street : the other somewhere on the site to be occupied by Temple Street. To these came the comedian Hallam, with a company of players from London. Their earliest announcements are to be found in Aris's *Birmingham Gazette ;* the " Playhouse in New Street," mentioned in 1741, is the shed on the site of modern Temple Street ; and the " Theatre in Smallbrook Street," advertised in 1747, is the booth in the Hinkleys. About the year 1730, a barn or woodshed in Castle Yard was used for performances of a crudely comic kind : the price of admission was 3d. a head, so we may assume that the entertainment was of a popular sort. The notices of the other places show that their repertoire was of a fair standard. For example, a performance was given, in 1743, of *The Mourning Bride*, which was followed by a selection of Brotherly Songs, given by a Mason. Dates are conjectural ; but there was a practice of advertising a play as " not acted here these twenty years," from which we can determine that plays of a good quality were being given in the town by 1730 at the least. These were in the Temple Street booth : Castle Yard was flourishing ten years later, and Smallbrook Street was set up about 1740.

The first place to be used as a regular theatre was a building in a back-yard off Moor Street. It was not constructed for dramatic purposes, but was converted, and it has been suggested that it was a rather makeshift erection. A scrutiny of one of its bills, quoted below, does not at all confirm this. Plays were given at Moor Street, on Monday, Wednesday and Friday evenings, from July to October, by a London company under the comedian, Richard Yates. The practice of bringing a London company out to the provinces when the Metropolitan theatres were closed for the summer continued for a long time. It was in use at the Theatre Royal at first, as the following notice shows :—

> " The Theatre Royal, in Drury Lane, not closing until Saturday the seventh instant, renders it impossible to open New Street until Friday, the thirteenth instant."

Performances at Moor Street were first announced by a drummer parading through the town ; and it was maliciously reported that Yates himself was known to take this office. The company grew conscious of its London origin, and begged to be excused the drum. Printed announcements were then used.

The earliest notice of a Moor Street play is in Aris's *Gazette*, and is worth quoting in full, except for the names of the cast :

By a Company of Comedians from London,

At the New Theatre in Moor Street,

The present Evening being the 29th of this instant, will be revived

THE TEMPEST
or the
INCHANTED ISLAND

As altered by Mr. Dryden and Sir William Davenant.
[here the cast given]

Concluding with a Grand Masque of
NEPTUNE AND AMPHYTRITE

No person can be admitted behind the Scenes, on Account of the Machinery. Boxes and Stage, 2/6 ; Pit. 2/- ; Balconies, 2/- ; 1st Gallery, 1/-, 2nd 6d. ; To begin punctually at 7 o'clock.   Vivat Rex.

This is an advertisement for a performance on the 20th of August, 1744. If Moor Street had two Galleries and machinery, it must have been a fairly substantial building. The machinery may not have been very extensive—the rule that no-one should go behind the scenes during a performance had been established by Queen Anne. The highest price is 2/6 ; which, in 1744, suggests a well-to-do patronage. The play and the masque indicate a theatre capable of fairly elaborate stage effect. We may note, too, the survival of the old custom of sitting on the stage.

The earliest play bills for Moor Street, are of the year 1753, but the press announcements indicate the early repertoire. For 1744, this included *The Provok'd Wife*, *Fair Rosamund* and *The Biter Bit*, in September ; *Love for Love*, with a pantomime, and *The Spaniard Outwitted*, in October ; *The Mourning Bride*, at the end of the same month ; and, on the 29th of October,

"for the Benefit of Mr. Francis Knowles Baker, who sustained great Losses by Fire . . . Othello."

All these programmes were filled out with dances, songs, farces and recitations ; but they represent a quite creditable repertoire. Apparently too, Moor Street was conscientious about costuming. An announcement for *Julius Caesar* says "in which the characters of the play will be dressed in the proper habits." There is a similar advertisement to the play *The Seige of Damascus*, in 1747.

It should be remembered that these buildings were not licensed for dramatic performances at all. A naïve and amusing fiction was used in order to give plays without coming into conflict with the law, rather like the modern sale of raffle tickets, which is made legal by marking the ticket as a receipt for a voluntary subscription. The performance was advertised as a concert of music, after which the players, freely, and for their own diversion, would give a play. The very first announcement for the Theatre Royal illustrates this :

> At the Theatre in New Street, Birmingham, this present Monday, June 20th, 1744, will be presented a Concert of Music—Boxes, 3/-; Pit, 2/-, Gallery, 1/-. Between the several parts of the Concert will be presented (gratis), by a Company of Their Majesties Comedians from the Theatre Royal in London, a Comedy called " As You Like It "—Touchstone, Mr. Yates—and an occasional Prologue to be spoken by Mr. Yates. To which will be added " Miss in Her 'Teens."

There was another form of unlicensed amusement, and one which caused great annoyance to the owners of regular theatres. At the larger public houses, concerts were given, which often included a dramatic entertainment. It may be supposed that the standard of this tap-room drama was not very high. Most likely the performance was in the nature of a modern Music Hall Variety, but on a smaller scale. However, they were popular and illegal. The owners of the Theatre Royal were to find them an undesirable competition, and to prosecute actions several times, against the owners of the various inns. Amongst those where performances were given were " The George and Dragon," " The Red Lion," in the Bull Ring, " The King's Head," Digbeth, and " The Roe Buck," Cox Street.

All this shows a growing interest in the drama ; and patronage grew to such an extent that Yates had a fine and substantial theatre built in King Street (formerly known as Queen's Alley) which was opened, by a Company of His Majesties' Servants in 1752. It was the principal place of entertainment until the building of the Theatre

Royal in 1774. In that year it was enlarged. It re-opened in 1775 :

> The Theatre in King Street, which has been rebuilt, and is now fitted up with new scenery, machinery, chandeliers, and every necessary decoration, will be opened for the first time on Monday next, the fifth of June, under the direction of Mr. Younger.

Hull and this Younger had had a company at King Street from 1762. When the Theatre Royal was built for Yates, a rivalry sprang up between him and his first theatre. Younger had King Street repainted in 1777 ; but it was shut by Justice Parsons after a few nights, possibly because of the practice of paying workmen with tickets.

Maddox re-opened King Street in 1779, but the days of the older playhouse had passed. In 1780 it was sold, and became Lady Huntingdon's Chapel. This curious metamorphosis is described by Hutton :—

> " Methodism still trod upon the heels of the players, for, in 1780, the spirit of the stage drooping, the itinerant preacher took possession of the Theatre in King Street."

Some of the playbills of this theatre remain ; and from them can be derived a good idea of the place which they advertise. Its season was like that of Moor Street, from early June until the end of September. Performances were begun at 7 o'clock, and prices were 3/-, 2/-, and 1/-. In 1775 eleven Shakespearean plays were given : *Henry VIII* was played twice, and the Dryden version of *The Tempest* six times. Plays by Otway, Goldsmith, Steele, Sheridan, Gay's *Beggar's Opera*, and a translation of *L'Avare*, make up another eleven performances. The programme in the following year was not of this quality.

Only eight plays by reputable dramatists were presented : these include three by Shakespeare, and Buckingham's *Rehearsal*. Many plays were given in this year which were favourites at the Theatre Royal, and frequently played during the next century. Among these are *Jane Shore*, *The West Indian*, *Guy of Warwick*, *Love in a Village*, *The Maid of the Mill*, *Tamerlane*, *The Irish Widow*, *Three Weeks After Marriage*, and *Bon Ton*. At this time, plays like *Braganza* were very popular—plays which were pseudo-classical or foreign tragedies. Production seems to have been lavish and spectacular, with every possible introduction of march, battle, song, dance and masque. The insertion of a hornpipe into *The Merchant of Venice*, or of a " Funeral Procession and Solemn Dirge " into *Romeo and Juliet*, was common, and, apparently, expected.

The Theatre Royal was opened in 1774. It was the last theatrical structure to be raised in Birmingham in the eighteenth century.

An Amphitheatre was set up in Stork Tavern Yard in 1802. Its existence was ephemeral and there is no record of what kind of performance it presented.

A more important Amphitheatre was built in Bradford Street during 1827—Ryan's. Equestrian drama was popular in the 'thirties, as can be seen from playbills of the time ; and " Ryan's Amphitheatre and New Grand Arena " was set up to cater for this taste. It was not licensed for drama, but apparently ignored the law ; for the manager of the Theatre Royal complained, in 1846, that it was giving dramatic entertainments. It was sold soon afterwards, and became, like King Street Theatre, a chapel.

The town's first Music Hall was the " George and Dragon," in Steelhouse Lane ; it was opened in 1840. It must be made clear that Music Hall was a title which was used literally : in such a place musical performances of a good standard were given. It was not until later in the century that a more debased form of entertainment was associated with these halls. The " George and Dragon " was the first stable building of this kind ; there had been a " Concert Booth and Opera House " on the Moseley Road as early as 1778, but this had been burned down in 1782.

In 1846 another Concert Hall opened, in Coleshill Street ; and in the same year a temporary erection in Queen's Street was used, illegally, for dramatic representation. The Committee of the Theatre Royal, always zealous in the prosecution of unlicensed theatres, took up this case ; and the use of the Queen Street Theatre was soon discontinued.

What is now the Prince of Wales Theatre was opened in 1856, as the " Birmingham Music Hall." The population of the town was increasing rapidly at this time, so the owners of the Theatre Royal were not unduly alarmed ; but they sent their solicitor to oppose an application for a licence for drama, which was made by the manager of the Music Hall in 1861. It was granted nevertheless.

The Shakespeare Rooms, a part of the Theatre Royal property, were frequently used for lectures, musical entertainments and the like. In 1856, the Manager of the Theatre Royal fitted up one of the rooms in these buildings with a stage ; and it was announced as the " Bijou Theatre."

Mr. Chute, of Bristol, had another Amphitheatre, in Moor Street, in 1866 : but its success was small, and he abandoned it three years later.

The popular music hall now began to appear. The

first in this tradition was "Day's Crystal Palace Concert Hall," which was part of the "White Swan" public house. In the following year, 1863, a similar place was opened in the Bull Ring : it was called "The London Museum Tavern and Concert Hall," but was familiarly known as "The Mucker." More sinister-sounding still is the title of the "Blood Tub," which was the popular name for the "Queen's Theatre Opera House," opened at Snow Hill in 1883. The last of these places, the Hippodrome in Hurst Street, was completed in 1895.

One major theatre alone was erected—the Grand, which opened in 1882. This, the last gesture of the nineteenth century, is now a dance hall ; but the original crimson and gold decorations, the heavy curtains and pelmets remain to show what a lavish theatre it was.

Most of these places of entertainment, by the very nature of their performances, have passed unnoticed by the town's dramatic critics. One journal, however, *The Birmingham Dramatic News*, 1884-5, deals with most of the music halls, as well as the theatres. The critic is not a very good one : he affects the unpleasant, slangy manner of the facetious Victorian, and hides his criticism under a load of cant terms and dubious jests. From him we learn that the Grand Theatre had a reputation for spectacular production, and for programmes which were entertaining rather than aesthetic. He remarks that :

"If he [the manager of the Grand] introduced a couple of niggers into the banqueting scene from Macbeth, a troupe of flying gymnasts in the Lady of Lions [*sic*], or made the Stranger sing a couple of comic songs, it is within the bounds of belief that the patrons of the Grand would not resent it."

The Theatre Royal, as we shall see, was giving its

attention largely to the spectacular, while the Prince of Wales presented comedy and light opera.

The impression which we receive of the music halls is not favourable. Crude entertainments were played to packed, alcoholic, vulgar houses. The critic himself, a rather vulgar person, comments on the poor fare with which the Birmingham audiences are pleased, and speaks acidly of the way in which a famous name would fill an auditorium, however poor the programme.

The tone of the town had changed since the cartographer wrote on his map in 1778 :

" This place has been, for a long series of years . . . superior to most Towns in the Kingdom for its elegance."

CHAPTER II

THE DIFFERENT BUILDINGS AND THEIR
MANAGERS

THE land on which the Theatre Royal was built
belonged to Mr. Inge, a member of an old local
family. On the tenth day of August, in the year 1773, a
group of men met at the Swan Inn and decided to write
to this gentleman asking him what rent he would accept
for a portion of ground adjoining New Street. The idea
of building a theatre had been in the air for some time—a
warning against such a project had been put in the local
press a few months previously. Nevertheless, the rent
asked proving reasonable, an agreement was drawn up, on
the tenth of the following September, between

W. Small, M.D., Tom Taylor junior, Esq., J. Green,
merchant, T. Wright, grocer, R. Goolden, silk mercer,
T. Faulconbridge . . . AND R. Yates, gent.

This agreement provided for " a Theatre, with proper
Stage, Traps, Boxes, Galleries, Staircases, Seats . . . "
and was to be ready by the following June. Its cost was
estimated at £1,500. The building was to be used for
theatrical performances only except by special permission
of the proprietors.

Richard Yates was the London comedian for whom the
theatre in King Street had been built in 1751. His new
house was built during the latter part of 1773 and the early

months of 1774, opening for its first production in June
of that year. Its appearance is uncertain. A picture
of the portico which was added in 1782 is often incorrectly
given. A study of early maps shows its position and
shape, while a tiny print in the great collection made by
H. S. Pearson appears to show the first front (*see Frontis-
piece*). It seems to have been a fine building, " upon
a suitable spot, an extensive plan, and richly ornam nted
with paintings and scenery."

It was built by Thomas Saul and painted by Mr. Colaboo.
The site was immediately to the east of the finest private
house in Birmingham, the house of Mr. Green, a well-
known dandy. The ground had formerly been known as
Greenwood's Cherry Orchard. It should be remembered
that the great industrial expansion of the town had not yet
begun. As a historian says :—

" Health and amusements are found in the prodigious
number of private gardens, scattered around
Birmingham, from which we often behold the father
returning with a cabbage, and the daughter with a
nosegay."

The proprietors were careful business men : thus much
is clear from their books. Having erected a substantial
theatre, they added two houses to the east side of it and
a road round the whole site. In 1777 they expanded again
and added a Coffee Room. It was in this year that they
suffered their first setback ; there was rivalry between
Yates and the manager of King Street. Both theatres
were closed.

" Perhaps it is unnecessary to inform our readers
that we have, among our public buildings, two theatres,
both of which are at this time shut up, owing to a
disagreement now unhappily subsisting between the
friends of the respective houses."

This is one suggested reason : another is that the two

managements had been in the habit of paying their workmen with theatre-tickets, a scandalous device which caused
great distress. However, the new theatre re-opened in
1779 under Miller of Shrewsbury who was manager for
two years. King Street tried to obtain sanction for the
title of " Royal " at this time, so the proprietors of the
new theatre instructed one of their members, Thomas
Faulconbridge, to solicit a similar bill in Parliament.
He claimed £105 expenses, but was not successful with
the Bill. There was some discussion in the House :—

" March 31st, 1777. Sir William (Bagot) declared
that if a Playhouse must be licensed, no Member could
hesitate that it ought to be granted to New Street
Theatre on every account. He said that he knew that
a comedian of King Street Theatre had stolen, last
Season, a Brace of Fat Bucks out of the Park of his
Friend, Sir Henry Bridgman. . . . He enlarged in general
on the pernicious tendencies of Playhouses in Manu-
facturing Towns.

" Mr. Burke : Why, I shall be free to say, I think the
Play will be the best Place that it is probable a Black-
smith's idle Moments will carry him to."

In 1780 the proprietors determined to have their
extended buildings nobly fronted. After enquiring the
price of Mr. Adams's Patent Stucco, finding it almost as
dear as stone, and rejecting it, they commissioned Mr.
Wyatt to construct a portico. This splendid structure
lasted until 1901, surviving two fires, and it was the chief
architectural pride of a street already handsome. A print
of it in 1805 is reproduced in Plate II. At the time of its
construction there were other alterations : the Gallery
Entrance was set at the back. It was soon proved best
to use this as an exit only—the Gods were a rough company—and a new way in was made from New Street. The
Coffee Room was boxed out and divided, " similar to those

in London." The houses were rented by one Charles Wildnay, and two other buildings turned into a warehouse by their first tenant, Abraham Pemberton. An insurance of £3,000 was effected. In 1792 the first dividends were paid out, which left " six shillings and three halfpences."

This prosperous beginning soon ended. At two o'clock on the morning of January 18th, 1792, the Theatre was set on fire by some incendiaries. There is an interesting print of the event, which appears to show the apprehension of a culprit, but this may have proceeded from the imagination of the artist since the proprietors offered a reward of £210 for information, and in vain. There had been several previous attempts, perhaps the work of mere hooligans, perhaps of that section of the town which had always been hostile to the theatre. The flames broke out in several places and the buildings were gutted : but the stout wall on Mr. Green's side, the rooms called the Shakespeare Tavern, and the new stone portico all survived.

The proprietors were undismayed. They voted sixteen guineas for those performers who had lost their possessions in the flames : twenty guineas were voted for " the Troops of the Royal Horse Guards . . . who attended on this melancholy occasion." The insurance companies offered £2,544/16/0. While re-building was in progress a former meeting house was used for performances under the name of the " Gentlemen's Private Theatre."

The proprietors took this opportunity to expand the estate. They leased nine houses from Jane Swaine on the south side of the Theatre. The portico was restored at a cost of £115, and an Assembly Room, and additional rooms for the tavern were constructed.

The new auditorium was 112 feet long. The stage, which was forty-eight feet deep, and fifty feet wide, with a proscenium aperture of thirty-eight feet, was apparently narrow for the house, and spaces at the sides were filled in with blank piers. The capacity of the house, which had two rows of Boxes and a Gallery, was 2,000 people, which meant nightly takings of £200 ; though Master Betty drew a crowd which yielded £268/4/0.

The new roof was of sufficient cunning to find mention in a book on carpentry published some years later. It was constructed by George Saunders, was 80 feet wide, and contained a workroom over the stage, 19 feet six inches wide and 18 feet high. This room was used for the operation of stage machinery, of which there was a large new stock. (Mr. Norton had been sent to examine the apparatus used at Drury Lane). This anxiety to imitate the Metropolis is frequently to be noted. The scenery which Norton recommended was painted by Messrs. Greenwood and Dixon. They also provided three sets of wings, and a painted drop-curtain. The tiers of seats were brave with elaborate columns, coloured pink, crimson, green and white. Each row of Boxes had its own Promenade ; and,—subtle attraction to the fastidious,—the different parts of the auditorium had separate entrances. Over the whole was a fan ceiling ; and illumination, formerly provided by tallow candles except on special occasions, now came from patent lamps, wax candles and a score of chandeliers. The Theatre must have been worthy of the high claims made for it by Hutton, who describes the fire and re-building thus :—

" One of our most elegant buildings cost, in 1774, 5,666l . . . But, on August 17th, 1791, while the practice of burning went unpunished, it was completely burned down, and the incendiaries were never discovered. The proprietors . . . have, in the compass of four years, erected, perhaps, the most commodious and superb theatre in the Three Kingdoms, London excepted, at the expense of 14,000 l., in the whole."

The proprietors advertised for a manager and received seven applications, including one from the prompter of Drury Lane, William Powell. The choice fell on W. M'Cready, father of the famous actor. He took the Theatre at an agreed rent of £500 and half the profits. The new house re-opened in May, 1794.

The theatrical season was from June to September. In 1798 M'Cready decided to become a full-time provincial manager, and hired the Theatre for the winter at a rent of £10. He did not use it for performances, because " as ours was not at that time a Royal Theatre, his season was restricted to 60 nights."

He was lessee until 1807, and his efforts were profitable. The huge debts incurred at the reconstruction of the Theatre were paid off, and in 1802 £330 was paid to Dixon to re-paint and gild the whole auditorium, with a further £100 for " a good front Drop." The elegant lamp-posts outside (*see Plate* III) were also repainted.

There had been difficulties, of course. While the rebuilding was going on, several companies of players had sought entry to the town and it had been necessary to resist them ; Yates had complained about the enlarging of the Theatre, and seems to have fought against it strongly ; the owners refused to give way to him, and he resigned. Equestrian performers came to town, and the proprietors declared that under no circumstances should Mr. Saunders' Company of Riders be allowed to use the Theatre. Some strange things were permitted, nevertheless. Astley hired the Theatre for £30 a week in November, 1802, to show " Grand Ballets, Grand Spectacles, Little Musical Pieces and Comic Pantomimes." In October, 1805, Dr.

Phillips displayed " Mechanical and Philosophical Experiments." Mr. Sutton gave an " Hydraulic Exhibition " in 1807.

It was early in this year that a second and successful attempt was made to call the playhouse Royal. There are still extant copies of " An Act to enable His Majesty . . . to grant Letters Patent for establishing a Theatre or Playhouse . . . in the Town of Birmingham." The date is the first of August, 1807. Perhaps it was this added dignity which induced the owners to raise their rent to £1,000.

M'Cready was not a mean man : he gave his services free at a charity performance to help the Blue Coat School pay off a debt of £800 and in 1796 a playbill bore the announcement, " Mr. M'Cready proposes that the entire Receipts of a Night should be appropriated for the Relief of Persons imprisoned for Small Sums," but this increase was more than he could support. He resigned his managership.

For a time the Theatre Royal stood empty. It was rented, from August 29th to 19th September, 1808, by Mr. Crisp, the manager of the Worcester, Northampton and Shrewsbury companies. After this came something new :

" Theatricals are to be introduced to this town during part of the winter season, which is certainly most favourable to them, and wherein they are found pleasant, and liberally encouraged in most large places . . . stoves are erecting to render the lobbies &c warm and comfortable."

The originator of this new season was Mr. Watson of the Cheltenham Company, who rented the Theatre Royal for one year, starting in November, 1808. He was not a very satisfactory tenant : he resented having to pay the twenty guineas which was his share of the Lamp and Scavenger

Levy, and he used illumination which damaged the painting ; nevertheless, he made profits.

In 1810, M'Cready took over again, on behalf of his son, who had had some experience of management at Newcastle and Chester. The young man made his first appearance on the stage that year, as Romeo, his performance being commended. His father was manager until 1812, and during this time he had put patent lamps over the stage, at a cost of £33, repaired the ropes of the drop-scenes, and carried out various other minor improvements.

The times were becoming less auspicious to dramatic enterprise. In Birmingham the growth of the Methodist and Quaker communities must have reduced the play-going public considerably. The nature of the town was changing : the industrial century was under way. When the first attempt had been made to have the Theatre licensed, in 1777, the aid of the Earl of Dartmouth was enlisted. He was known to be favourably inclined towards the stage ; it was under his lenient chamberlaincy that the minor theatres developed in the twenties and thirties. Writing to him, Matthew Boulton said :—

" Of late years, Birmingham hath been much visited by Persons of Fashion, and it is some inducement to prolong their stay when their evenings can be spent in a commodious airy Theatre."

In July, 1781, Lord Torrington visited Birmingham :

" By seven o'clock we were at the Play-House, which has been lately built, and become Royal : and it is now both within and without very commodious, with one Gallery and one row of upper Boxes, which give a snug and comfortable look . . . this front should be much admired for its neatness and elegance. The Play was almost as well performed as in London. . . .

We returned home before the Farce began, very melancholy, as Mr. P. intends to leave us to-morrow morning."

At about this time Hutton stated, in his *History of Birmingham*, "that about thirty-six of the inhabitants keep carriages for their own use : and near fifty have country houses."

The patronage of lords was now rarer ; Elliston, who was lessee in 1813, sought to capture the fancy of a better public by the institution of a fashionable evening.

"One evening of the week to be considered fashionable for theatrical amusements. On this evening, without inconvenience, perhaps, to any individual, an expectation might be held out that the best company of Birmingham and its neighbourhood would be collected at the Theatre . . . all persons coming to the Theatre on the Friday would be . . . surrounded by those they might be pleased to meet."

This Elliston was a great advertiser and showman, and of an impressive presence, as Charles Lamb bears witness :

"Wherever Elliston walked, sate, or stood still, there was the theatre. He carried about with him his pit, boxes and galleries, and set up his portable playhouse at the corners of streets, and in the market-places. Upon flintiest pavements he trod the boards still ; and if his theme chanced to be passionate, the green baize carpet of tragedy spontaneously rose beneath his feet."

Nevertheless, the performances given at this time were of a very poor quality and on one occasion the stage was turned into a field of corn in order to demonstrate Dobb's Reaping Machine. Around this unpromising subject was written a farce called *Fortune's Frolic*. Elliston was hiring the Theatre week by week,

"The allowance to be for three nights only per week. This condition arises out of the unanimous opinion of the Committee that the Town does not require, and may not support a more frequent Exhibition."

By sheer showmanship, Elliston made the Theatre pay its way; so much so, that the stage and scenery, which were in a dilapidated state, were repaired at a cost of £1,400. The Assembly Rooms were let out to all sorts of people, and the Tavern and Billiard Rooms must have shown a good return; but it is remarkable, in the depressed times, that Kean took £264 at a benefit performance in 1814.

Bunn became manager in 1819. He was faced with a disaster almost at once. On the sixth of January, 1820, soon after the performance was over fire again broke out inside the building. As before, the portico and the surrounding property—by now swollen to thirteen house- and a small shop—withstood the flames, but the auditorium was burned out.

All but two of the original Trustees were dead; the remaining Proprietors decided to sell out.

A new group of Proprietors was formed at once, and set re-building operations afoot to such good purpose that the Theatre was ready in seven months. An expert from London, Mr. Owen, constructed the stage: an iron roof was erected, but soon proved unsuitable; the owners spent many harassed months trying to sell it, and at last disposed of it for scrap. An iron cradle at the back of the stage broke, while work was going on, and a labourer was killed, six others being injured. The Committee was troubled by the sensational press accounts of this accident, for the *Globe* reported that "Twenty-six poor fellows were either killed or dreadfully injured, and six are ascertained to be dead."

Bunn was placed on the Committee and gave advice on

the re-building. This proceeded so well that in August, 1820, it was announced :—

"To the Proprietors and Friends . . . the Theatre will certainly open on Monday next . . . no Inconvenience can arise from the Dampness or the unpleasant smell of Paint, as no Plaister has been employed in the Theatre . . . the Walls being all battened with Wood covered with Canvas. Great Pains also have been taken, under the Direction of Mr. Sylvester of London, to assure complete and adequate Ventilation throughout the Theatre."

A word may be said here about the use of gas. (A full account of the lighting of the Theatre Royal will be found in Chapter IV). The first use of gas for illumination may have been at the Boulton and Watt works, Soho, to celebrate the Peace of Amiens, in 1802. Matthew Boulton was a member of the Theatre Royal Committee and may have encouraged the use of gas in the playhouse when it was still considered a dangerous novelty. The Birmingham Gaslight Company was formed in 1819, and probably the first main was laid in New Street in 1820, so the Theatre was able to have its new auditorium illuminated in the most up-to-date manner.

The new house opened bravely enough, but Bunn was lamenting a loss of £500 at the end of his first season. The Committee charged him only £300 rent, limited the season to its former length, May to October, and stopped winter theatricals.

In 1821 there was a deficit of £13,000. There was no money even for scenery, and Bunn himself made "three horizon flats and a tomb." One expense only was undergone, and one which shows again that provincial desire to emulate the Metropolis which has already been remarked,— the "dish and burner of the Drury Lane Chandelier" was sought and installed. By the end of the year the position was serious. The season had been poor, Bunn was heavily in arrears with his rent, and creditors were pressing the Committee. Then someone offered to buy the White Elephant—the iron roof. It realised £275, and the Committee, heartened by this, plunged into new expense. The warehouse behind the Theatre was bought for £1,700 and some new Boxes were built. At the same time, Bunn earned a reprimand by cutting and altering the stage, but he was allowed to extend it towards the Pit by another 3' 6", and even to bring horses on to it, though the result was a good deal of damage. His lease expired in 1822, when his debts to the Committee were £498/16/10. He offered to sell all his scenery and dramatic library, and the catalogue makes interesting reading. A copy with a valuer's notes is extant, and from the frequent remark " Good for nothing " it is clear that Bunn's possessions were in a very poor way. The Wardrobe is a collection of shoddy magnificence and tinsel splendour : the entire sale of 762 lots, many of them large pieces of scenery, made only a little over six hundred pounds.

A man called Warde was lessee until 1826, and of him it can only be said that he made a fair profit and that during his managership candles and lamps were banished entirely from the Theatre. He was followed by Brunton of Plymouth, who began by making a loss of some six hundred pounds. He sought the patronage of the Proprietors " in these unpropitious times," but met with such little success and was so heavily in debt, that he offered to insure his life and hand the policy to the Committee. All his seasons were failures : he never came within £2,000 of Warde's receipts. In a pathetic letter, he offered the Committee 3/6 in the £. The Committee demanded 5/-. Despite his misfortunes, he seems to have been a man of integrity. Macready also records how, after having given a performance of *Hamlet* he found that the takings, amounting to £200, had been stolen. This was during Brunton's lesseeship yet Macready's words are : " At Birmingham, now under . . . Mr. Richard Brunton, a truly worthy man."

In 1828, Lewis, from the Liverpool Theatre took a lease for three years. He took steps to attract the public, and the Theatre being in a very dilapidated state, determined to improve it. The columns of the auditorium were picked out in green and white, at four shillings a time ; the seats of the Lower Boxes were stuffed with hair, and the lower tier was covered with crimson moreen ; but the audiences were no larger. In November 1830, Lewis wrote that the " depressed state of the times and the very slender patronage " obliged him to withdraw. His successor, Watson of the Cheltenham Theatre, had a short period of good fortune. He wrote :

"Indeed, had not public measures taken the turn which they appear now to do, I certainly should consider that most Theatres would be best done away with altogether."

Our next news of him is from Warwick Gaol, where he was imprisoned for debt.

Fraser was temporary lessee in 1833, and is chiefly famous for having engaged the Italian violinist, Niccolo Paganini, for three nights, and then having vanished with the profits on the third. This rogue was followed by two more. Fitzgibbon and Wightman took a joint lease but their audiences were small, except when, on one occasion, Wightman's creditors appeared in strength and created an uproar throughout the performance. Wightman retired at the end of a year, and Fitzgibbon took a lease

Plate II

CIRCA 1805

for three years, being required by the Committee to pay his rent in advance. It was said of him that he was only seen outside the Theatre on a Sunday, as on that day the High Sheriff could not arrest him for debt.

The Committee learned with pleasure that he had surrendered his lease at the end of 1835, and the new tenant, Armistead of Liverpool, was welcomed. He went the way of the others quickly enough. Early in 1837 he was arrested for debt. When his case came up at Warwick Assizes, Baron Park, who was presiding, released some of the jury to go and vote in the North Warwick Elections. Armistead's solicitor objected; and by the time the jury was made up he was preparing to go home, and refused to stay. The manager was returned to prison, which left the Committee in a difficult plight, for Armistead had set a watchman in the Theatre and no-one was able to get past him. The Committee consulted a legal adviser and found that they might not use force. Early one morning they made a stealthy entry. Armistead was released from prison on the formal surrender of all claims to the Theatre.

Monro of Leicester managed the Theatre for the next two years, and, by giving entertainment which was popular rather than dramatic, paved the way for his stage manager, Mercer Simpson, who succeeded him. Monro introduced " menagery " spectacles, which included tigers, monkeys and an elephant. Finding that audiences were turbulent, and that there were dangerous riots in the Gallery, he arranged to have police in attendance at all performances. The animals had damaged the stage, so a new one was put down. The property was, in fact, much improved, so that Simson, who took over in 1840, had a fair chance of prosperity.

He followed Monro's lead, displaying American Horses, lions, etc., and was the founder of the tradition of Christmas Pantomime at the Royal. The Committee was pleased with his success, " in view of the present ruinous state of theatrical property." Nevertheless, they had further worries at the time for a number of small houses in the town were applying for licences for drama, and illegal performances were being given at various taverns. The proprietors took action, and notices were served on four public houses. A theatre in Queen Street was closed, and Ryan's Amphitheatre was refused permission for dramatic performances. In 1854 there was serious opposition, when Tonks, the owner of Bingley Hall, was allowed a licence for drama ; but the venture failed, as the accoustics of the building were unsuitable.

Except for this abortive competition, the next few years brought nothing but prosperity to the Theatre Royal. The Committee began to feel its position and voted a subscription of two guineas towards the establishing of a school behind the Theatre. When Queen Victoria visited Birmingham in 1858, the proprietors spent £36/12/2 on the erection of a balcony in New Street, and they, and their families, to the total of a hundred and fifty people, sat therein, adding to the patriotic fervour of the hour. The buildings were illuminated to mark the marriage of the Prince of Wales, in 1863.

There were various alterations in the Theatre during this period. About £600 was spent on decoration, drainage and a hot-air heating system. The behaviour of the gallery crowd made it necessary to reinforce the stairs, " to withstand the frequent rushes " ; and spikes were set on top of the partition which separated the orchestra from the Pit. A fire broke out in the room over the stage in

1854 and did £40 worth of damage. Part of the property which adjoined the Theatre and had been used as a distillery, was rebuilt, with new houses and offices. A new stage was laid down in 1868 and the auditorium overhauled. The fire at the Haymarket in 1867 caused some alarm, and a new exit was built by way of safeguard. Refreshment rooms were built by Simpson's son, who became lessee in 1864. They were not a financial success ; and in 1869 the Committee received " complaints of the establishment of a Refreshment Bar within the old Box Entrance, and of the Character of Female Visitors thereat."

Simpson the younger had a difficult beginning in all respects. There was competition now from three theatres and three music halls, and the Lord Chamberlain was unwilling to renew the Patent, because he was not satisfied with the way in which liquors were sold in the bars. In 1874 the Corporation wanted to raise the level of Queen Street, and there was trouble over compensation—the Committee wanted £2,150, and this aroused public opposition. Then the insurance companies, alarmed at all the theatrical disasters, wanted to rescind their business with the Royal. It was indignantly pointed out that " There is not a Theatre in the Kingdom where more precautions are taken for safety from fires," and these are enumerated—a tank on the roof, taps on the stage and a night watchman—clearly the lessons of the past had been learned. The proprietors were further anxious at " the recent fire and fearful loss of life at Vienna," and promptly experimented to find out how quickly the audience could leave the Royal in case of emergency. It was found that even a full house of 1,200 could leave in a very short space of time.

Simpson the younger took careful stock of the auditorium in 1875 and then applied for a major alteration. He wanted the Pit lowered and extended back under the boxes, and pointed out that :—

> " a great improvement will be affected [*sic*] by the lowering of the Pit, much annoyance often occurring to the Lower Box Audience by the contiguity of the Pit Audience."

This was carried out. The Pit was extended, and its capacity increased from 600 to 1,200. A comparison of figs. v and vi will show the character of the alteration. Fig. vii shows the Pit itself, just before the Theatre was demolished at the beginning of the present century.

The other major improvements were, first, the removal of the elaborate columns of the 1820 rebuilding. They were replaced by iron girders in the roof, and the improvement was especially noticeable on the stage, where large scenic effects had been hampered by the presence of two vertical supports. Secondly, a fire-proof drop-curtain was added. The reason for this preoccupation with fire will be apparent if an examination is made of the repertoire of the century; fireworks, guns, flaming ruins are all commonplace, while pans of blue and red fire were set off during pantomimes at frequent intervals. Thirdly, in 1885 (up to which year all lighting had been by gas), an engine-room was made for the generation of electricity.

> " The footlights are entirely electric, so that the members of the orchestra will not, in future experience that heat which necessarily arises from the use of gas."

Finally, the room over the stage was removed, and the " gridiron " taken up 18 ft., so that drop scenes could all be raised easily.

These are the main changes which took place before the demolition. The last decade of the nineteenth century was a troubled one for the Theatre Royal. Simpson complained that the town's three theatres made his profits suffer. He attempted to form a syndicate with the rival houses in 1890, but without success. Five years later there was again difficulty in getting the patent renewed. The matter was now in the hands of the local magistrates, and not those of the Lord Chamberlain. The new authority declared that the Theatre was overcrowded and alterations had to be made to the staircases.

Simpson had sublet to Charles Dornton in 1892. The latter was a former member of the Birmingham stock company; he had been on tour, and made a fine profit out of a play called *The Silver King*. He died in 1900, and the managership was taken over by his wife.

It was now becoming clear that the buildings were obsolete. The Boxes were so designed that it was not possible to see the stage from many of them—perhaps this peculiarity dated from the time when the Theatre had been a place for the gathering of a fashionable society, and not the place of relaxation for an industrial populace. At the end of 1901 there was a great closing performance and then the workmen began to demolish Mr. Wyatt's portico, which had stood for a hundred and twenty years. The two plaques of Garrick and Shakespeare which had ornamented it were purchased by Philip Rodway, and built into an interior wall of the new structure. The sale of properties at which they were bought shows that, in spite of the difficult times, the managers had done their best by the Theatre. The new switchboard had cost £140, and the dressing rooms were all elaborately fitted up. A survey of the property in 1898 had valued it at £8,000 per annum. In 1899, when the proprietors determined to sell out their Deed of Association, which had been drawn up in 1834, being obsolete, their balance was over six thousand pounds.

There were difficulties over the new building. It was announced, before the old was down, that it would be six storeys high, Spanish Renaissance style, built of Carrara stone and buff terra-cotta. Its capacity was to be 3,400, and it would cost £30,000. This was not carried out. The Theatre finally emerged with five storeys, built in the style of George III, with an elevation of 69 ft. and a height of 75 ft. It had a Pit, Dress Circle, Upper Circle and Gallery, with an accommodation of 2,200. Its cost was about £50,000.

Chapter III

THE AUDIENCE

THE Theatre Royal opened, in 1774, with a brilliant and fashionable audience : a few youths who came in ordinary dress were criticised, but it must be said at once that the Birmingham audiences, especially those of the Gallery, were notoriously bad. There are numerous references to this, and many reasons for it. The town has always been an industrious one, even before it could be called an industrial one. Hutton gives us a vivid likeness of it in the eighteenth century, and tells how he was awakened from sleep at three o'clock every morning by the din of hammers and anvils. The Gallery audience must have been made up very largely of working people, whose manners would be rough, and although this element would not be noticeable at first, because early prices were prohibitive, it was certainly well established throughout the Theatre by the nineteenth century. It could behave well for its favourites :

"Acted Macbeth, yes, well. The audience, the Birmingham audience, gave me a reception such as I have never witnessed out of London, and very, very rarely even there. That stillness that followed, every word ringing on the ear, was really awful."

This was for Macready, in 1849. Such behaviour in that

century was rare, as we shall see, but in the seventeen-hundreds an audience must generally have had a fair number of respectable people in it. We may recall Matthew Boulton's letter to the Earl of Dartmouth in which, as the chief reason for having a licensed Theatre in Birmingham, he speaks of the number of people of fashion who come to the town in the summer. The early repertory, too, like that of King Street and Moor Street, suggests a reasonably well-educated audience. At the same time it should be remembered that the town had a large nonconformist community, and the solid Shakespearian programmes of the early days may have been designed with an eye to opposition. Hostility was certainly strong. The results of a poll, taken in 1777 in connection with the application for a licence, showed 1,468 against a theatre, 124 for it, 192 indifferent and 665 not at home.

Early prices were too high for many. In 1790, they ranged from 3/- for a Box to 1/- in the Gallery. Similar prices were being charged at King Street fifty years earlier. A shilling for a Gallery seat in 1790 seems a great deal, especially when we see that the same seat cost sixpence in 1910. It must be presumed that the Theatre was only patronised by the well-to-do at this time, though there is a suggestion of a rough Gallery in the following announcement for 1796 :

"The Circulation of Gallery Tickets having been objected to by the Magistrates, and other Gentlemen, as being in many Instances injurious ... Mr. Mac'Cready has agreed that none shall be issued during the present Season."

In those days the Theatre often gave a play at the request of some visiting or resident persons of position. Perform-

40

ances were bespoke by the High Sheriff, the Officers and men of the 6th Dragoon Guards, and the King's Royal Hussars. On one famous occasion, a play was performed at the request of Lord Nelson. In August 1802, the Admiral attended the Theatre with Sir William and Lady Hamilton, and saw *The Merry Wives of Windsor.* On the following day *King Henry IV* was given at his request. The visit of Lord Torrington in 1781 and the dignified approval of that nobleman have already been quoted, as has the establishment of a " fashionable night " in 1813 by Elliston ; while in the early part of the nineteenth century, performances were patronised by the Duchess of Kent and by Princess Victoria.

The first players were all from London. M'Cready would bring down famous actors and actresses, who would attract a good class of audience. After he gave up the practice of importing all his talent from the City and relied on strollers to make up a stock company, the standard of playing, and of spectator, began to decline. There was always a strong tendency to imitate the ways of fashionable London in this newly-important industrial town. Indeed, the presence of a blank copy of a Drury Lane Shareholder's Certificate of 1810 suggests that those of the Royal may have been modelled on it. The shareholders themselves were solid men, merchants, lawyers and doctors, and their patronage was often sought, and advertised, by the managers when houses were poor.

Even in the early days, the unruly element of the town found its way into the Gallery. The Theatre faced on to the finest street in the place, but at the rear lay the darkest slum. A few moments' walk from New Street brought one to the notorious Hinkleys, where, until late in the nineteenth century, the policemen walked in threes.

Undesirables from this area came to the Theatre and in 1788 the following advertisement was published :—

> A Reward will be paid by the Manager to any Person who will discover the Ruffians who have thrown, or shall hereafter throw, Bottles, Plates, Apples &c. at the Actors and upon the Stage, during and after the Performance.

An announcement on a Play Bill of 1814 indicates that this turbulent audience was taking ironwork from the Gallery. Our best account of these unruly spectators is given in a weekly of the period 1822–3, *The Theatrical Looker-On*. This work will be quoted so extensively in these pages that a brief description of it is merited. It was anonymous, but the writer was clearly a witty and well-educated person of leisure. He was opinionated, at times injudicious, but always stimulating. He was very frank with everyone, actor and spectator alike. There were several attempts to find out who he was, with a view to a public horse-whipping, but his identity is lost and he appears to have remained unwhipped.

His journal, which was concerned solely with the Theatre Royal, confirms the suggestion that, by the beginning of the century, audiences were deteriorating. He speaks of public taste :

> " The appetite of the public is so sick and depraved that the best writings of our dramatic poets almost invariably fail to attract an audience."

In a similar vein, criticising the play *Timour the Tartar* :

> " Lots of blue and red fire in the last scene . . . is charm enough for the Birmingham Gallery ; they have a knack of wishing every head empty that is fuller than their own."

Strangely enough these people were prudish, for a female tight-rope artiste, whose actions caused a display of limb,

42

was received doubtfully. This is odd in an audience which prevented the *Looker-On* from giving an account of an evening's programme, because " it was their sovereign will not to permit us to hear a syllable of the first two acts." At the best of times, the play was likely to be interrupted by " bawling recognitions . . . much edifying whistling . . . nut shells and orange-peel," while the same critic gives the following description of a crowded house :—

> " In the Dress Boxes we had a happy mixture of fish, flesh and fowl—the fish-woman, butcher and poulterer—the thief with one hand on the crimson cushion of the Box, and the other in his neighbour's pocket—gin, water, or the mixture, running down from the upper to the lower Boxes, plentifully supplying all empty hats—more oaths than Babel ever knew, and no place but Birmingham could utter—there must have been six hundred people in the Boxes only, and at least a score of lice to a man."

We can now understand the anxiety which the owners of a theatre would have to bear. The proprietors of the Royal apparently displayed an absurd caution when, in 1829, William Cobbett wanted the use of the Theatre to lecture on Currency, and they told him that it could not be hired out for political purposes ; but this solicitude is understandable in view of the rowdy elements which were in the town. For so innoccuous a meeting as the Annual Dinner of the Loyal and Constitutional Association, it was necessary to provide £100 security, and two guarantors. Political feeling always tended to run high in Birmingham. The audience of creditors who attended Armistead's benefit has been mentioned. The same evening ended with a display of anti-Tory feeling.

Riotous houses could be dangerous. In 1838, the Gallery was led to believe that a favourite acrobat, Neno the Gnome Fly, was being cheated of his wages. The benches were torn up and hurled into the Pit, the chandeliers smashed, and the house stripped.

The bread which accompanied these circuses was in the form of apples, oranges and ginger-beer, noisily sold by large women with baskets. This was a universal nuisance, for the Drury Lane audiences of 1849 were

> " constantly disturbed between the acts by women with huge and clumsy baskets, filled with apples, oranges, nuts, ginger beer, bottled stout and bills of the play."

At the Royal it was customary to roll a barrel of beer into the Gallery from a neighbouring inn. Later in the century bars were installed and became the haunt of women of the town. The Theatre had always attracted prostitutes, but it was claimed that they infested the box-lobbies only, presumably as more monied custom was to be found there.

The audience was not only noisy, but capricious. When Macready took his farewell benefit, he wrote :—

> " Acted King Lear to such a house as never was seen before in Birmingham. Acted my best, but the house, though attentive, was too full to enjoy the play."

The opening of a new music hall in the same year affords the Royal proprietors no anxiety :—

> " a new Music Hall has been opened, but the rapid increase in population fully makes up for any attraction which this place of Amusement may have."

On the other hand, this comment was written in the Diary of the money-taker at the Pit Entrance :—

> " 22 May, 1862. Miss Jones Benefit . . . As You Like It . . . when the doors were opened, there was not a Soul at Pit or Gallery for several minutes."

When the Gods came, they still gave tongue. Barry Sullivan had to ask for quiet after giving two acts of

Richard III virtually in dumb show, in 1866. The noise was not always caused by dislike of the actor,—Sullivan was popular enough,—but there were private fights in the Gallery, which often began with a struggle for the " centre-knob," a brass knob in the middle of the front rail, which was a place of honour. Two men would begin to jostle for this, and the strife might spread to the entire Gallery audience. With the custom of charging only half price for admission after nine o'clock, it would come about that a stream of rough individuals, many of whom would be drunk already, would pour into the Gallery, and begin noisy comments, greetings, struggles and further tipplings. Even the Pit cannot have been unexceptionable. Simpson had it lowered because the " contiguity of the Pit audience " was annoying to the people in the Lower Boxes.

The last story of ruffianism we have is from a daily newspaper of 1884 when some scoundrels, knowing the power of the Gallery, molested a pantomime artiste outside the theatre. They demanded money, threatening that if it were refused they would see that the performer was hissed off the stage on the next night. The writer of the account suggests that a good spell on the treadmill might act as a deterrent. His tone implies that such perse-cution is by now considered an outrage and that the days of the old Gods were passing. In the twentieth century, audiences improved here as elsewhere, though the town has never lost its reputation for roughness.

In considering these stories of ill behaviour, it should be realised what type of entertainment was showing, and at what time it was shown. From the earliest days to the present century, the curtains of the Theatre Royal have gone up at about seven o'clock. There was, in fact, no alteration until the nineteen-thirties, when the time was changed to half-past the hour. On this subject the manager remarked, in 1929 : "I don't think anyone would be deceived into thinking that a show beginning at half-past seven, and ending at ten is longer than one beginning at a quarter past seven and ending at a quarter to ten." In the nineteenth century performances would last until after eleven, and if some London actor came down, the curtain might not come down until two in the morning. As early as 1825 there are complaints of the practice of cramming too much into a benefit bill, for, after eleven, the actors were tired and the audience became restive. The repertoire, too, was conducive to noise. From about 1815 onwards, the characteristic shape of a programme was :—

(*a*) A curtain raiser, usually a farce.

(*b*) The main play, perhaps a five-act tragedy.

(*c*) A dance, or acrobatic display.

(*d*) A melodrama.

This was interspersed with songs, recitations and sketches. The main play might be an equestrian drama, or full of armies, flames and emotion. The farces were crude, boisterous, vulgar and suggestive.

Prices of admission have already been mentioned. The following comparison may be of interest :—

1790 : Boxes, 3/- ; Pit, 2/- ; Gallery, 1/-.

1925 : Upper Circle, 2/4 ; Pit, 1/6 ; Gallery, 1/-.

In 1925, it was possible to hire a Box for 45/-, but some of the prices were the same as a century and more before. This supports the contention that the audiences became

46

more popular as time went on. A shilling in 1790 was a good sum. In 1827 there was this plea :—

" It is the decided general opinion of a great class of play-goers, particularly men of business, of whom, for the greater part, the Birmingham people are composed, as well as clerks in mercantile houses, who are occupied until nine o'clock, and sometimes later, and who enjoy a play, [that] the barrier is the price—now, if half-price were allowed, or at least the admission to the Boxes, and to the Pit, 1/6 after 9 o'clock. . . . "

The Gallery price was reduced to 6d. in the 1840's, and this was the standard bottom price until the Great War.

We can also take into account the other side of this matter of finance—the profits and losses of the proprietors, whose fluctuations indicate the state of theatricals in the town, and in the provinces in general. The 1773 building is said to have cost £5,600, and although the Deed of Agreement only says £1,500, the larger figure is the more probable. The portico alone cost " over £750 "—there is no more specific record. Reconstructing the shell after the fire of 1792 meant an outlay of £3,000. The new proprietors, who took over in 1820, had a bad start : they paid £8,331 to the former owners, £18,980 for building, and quote their total outlay, in odd terms, as " about £27,313/4/2." With these basic expenses in mind, we can examine the record of profit and loss.

The first fifteen years are a tale of expenditure only, and there was no balance. The first was at the end of 1789, £189/7/6. This is consistent until the fire in 1792. The profits of the first season after this were £816/1/2—a very large sum, but the Committee were £1,400 in debt still. Their funds never reach the right side of the folio again. £1,000 was borrowed to alter the stage mechanism in 1814, before the debts from the rebuilding had been paid up.

In 1820, at the second fire, the proprietors withdrew. They took £3,967/2/6 with them from the insurance companies, and £8,331 from the new owners. There follows a depression ; audiences were poor, managers were ineffective at best, dishonest at worst. Not until 1831 was the tremendous debt of the purchase and rebuilding paid off, and during this time there were many calls on shares, and increases in rent, though the latter was not always paid. At the end of 1831 there is a favourable balance of £450/4/3. This was reduced to an adverse figure of some sixty pounds by the defaulting of Fraser and the repainting, upholstering and repairs to the Theatre and the Box Lobbies, whose windows the " Schoolboys had broken." In spite of the management of Armistead and Fitzgibbon, there was a credit of £707 by 1836—perhaps because of the frequent hiring of the Shakespeare Rooms, which were very popular. Thereafter, from £600 to £1,000 is in the balance, until the selling out in 1899. The balance was then £6,106/1/2 and the property was valued at £8,000 p.a.

Plate III

An etching of the Theatre Royal about 1825. The alterations made after the fire of 1820 may be seen if this is compared with Plate II. The most obvious change is in the roof, which now appears entirely flat.

Chapter IV

THE STAGE AND SCENERY

THE STAGE

O F the first stage which the theatre had, we know nothing but what the Agreement of 1773 tells us. This document specifies " a Theatre with proper Stage, Traps, &c.", of which the only significant detail is " Traps." If the assumption made in Chapter II about the position of the first building is correct, its stage must have been very small. Nevertheless, it seems that here, as at the other early theatres of the town, a good deal of machinery was used. A programme for Moor Street Theatre in 1744 refers to machinery, and announces that patrons may not go behind the scenes because of it. The repertoire of the King Street Theatre suggests large scenic effects. Marches, masques and battles were a common ingredient of the plays, and the songs which were given between the acts were probably to allow the scene-shifters time to move heavy pieces. The repertoire of the first Royal building is of the same calibre.

The theatre was burned down in 1792. When it was rebuilt, a stage 50 ft. wide and 48 ft. long was laid down. It was said that as the theatre was now wider, the stage was rather narrow for the house—there were blank piers on either side of it to fill up, as the auditorium was some 80ft.

wide—so perhaps its dimensions were based on those of the old stage.

This stage, and its scenery, suffered from the man-handling of large pieces. In the early nineteenth century, England was far behind the rest of Europe in the science of scene-shifting; machinery was used abroad, while the work was all done by hand at home. The scene-shifters at the Theatre Royal were not of a very high order. We have some pungent comments among the dramatic criticism of a play-goer of 1825. He complains of scenes left out on the stage—" Burlington Arcade being replaced by the King's Bench, as in *Giovanni in London*."

Scenes were left half-set—the actors might find themselves in half a wood and half a palace, or on a stage of which one side was a likeness of Cumnor Place, the other of Kenilworth Castle. Not only were the men responsible for this chaos noisy and incompetent, but quite often visible, too :

" In the window of every house, and at the door of every street, we have the physiognomy of some ill-looking chap thrust into perspective."

There was machinery for the moving of scenes and pro-perties, but it was not used, so that there were long delays, and the material deteriorated. As early as 1814, the proprietors had informed their manager that it would be better " if the scenery were drawn in upon rolers [*sic*] instead of lengthways, as they were at present."

Damage went on, nevertheless, and in 1821, repairs to the stock cost £82.

The nature of this scenery may be gathered from a catalogue of a sale, made in 1825 by Bunn, to pay off his debts. (*See* Appendix).

In the lists is a large number of sinking, breaking and

flying pieces, with various cataracts and fountains. Trick stage effects were very popular throughout the century. Many of these pieces are marked by a valuer, and are clearly in a very bad condition. They suffered, no doubt, from the handling of the workmen. The stage suffered from the same cause, and also from the showing of equestrian drama, popular from about 1820 onwards. By 1842, the stage was dangerous, and a new one was built by a Mr. Aldridge. The work cost £317/14/6. The exact size of the new stage is unknown, but probably, in view of the complaints about the narrowness of its predecessor, and the spectacular productions which the audiences in Birmingham demanded, it was wider.

This stage lasted for twenty-two years—an astonishing survival when the performances of the period are considered. It was replaced in 1864.

Until 1885, when they were supplanted by girders in the roof, two pillars, somewhat in the manner of those which supported the Elizabethan " Heavens," had marred the Royal stages. When they were at last removed, it was found that scene-shifting was much simpler.

A fire-proof drop-curtain was added in 1887, and our last sight of the things behind it is in 1902, with the sale of properties, before the old building is demolished. The catalogue is bizarre. It includes a number of pantomime rats, a zinc bath, a few large sea-horses, a large, octagonal fountain with four hundred jets, some Sheraton furniture, and " a fine old property barge." There is also a great mass of pantomime properties and scenery. But the sale was a dismal affair. A Moorish palace was sold for £3, and an engraving of Alfred the Great was knocked down for 6/—" just after his millenary, too."

THE SPECTACLE

The Victorian age is notorious for its love of spectacular scenes and staging. It has been suggested that this was connected with its many new discoveries—that it was childishly proud of its advances, and so developed a love of exhibition of all kinds.

Spectacular sets at the Theatre Royal date from before the nineteenth century, and are chiefly connected with two kinds of play which might be termed the aquatic and the incendiary. As early as 1795 " A grand view of the British Fleet riding at Anchor," was shown, though this was probably effected by a painted back-cloth and moving models rather than by a tank of water. In the next year, *The Tempest* was produced " with a Storm and Shipwreck in Act Two." 1796 also saw a pantomime production which clearly indicates the early love of elaborate staging. It was called *Harlequin Mariner*, and in it Columbine was released from the Cavern of Vice, " in which are personified Avarice, Murder, Envy, Indolence and Drunkenness. The Scene is succeeded by a most magnificent View of the Temple of Virtue."

A play on the story of Pyramus and Thisbe, produced in 1798, had a scene showing " The Tomb of Ninus by Moonlight," which probably means that " Ninny's Tomb " was in the form of a two-dimensional flat, or simply of a pyramid painted on a back-cloth.

Really heavy staging does not appear until the following century when equestrian drama became popular in the second decade. 1814 and 1815 were glorified by *A Real Horse Race !* and *A Real Fox Chace* [*sic*] *!* In these years, *Timour the Tartar* first took his rattling canter across the creaking boards of the Theatre Royal and the equine aristocracy, a group of horses trained in the *haute école*, danced to a minuet by Haydn. In 1815 a tank of water was certainly used, for with the Horse came the Dog, in the famous play *Caravan* :

> " The last Scene represents a most beautiful and picturesque View of a River and Cascade of real Water. The Dog leaps from a stupendous Precipice into the River, and preserves the Life of the Child Julio."

The tank was in comic employ next year. A pantomime, *Harlequin Horner*, was shown, in which the characters enter a booth built on a frozen river :

> " The Booth changes to a Steam Boat, the Ice breaks, they fall into the Water, a large Fish rises with a Car attached, they get into the Car, and are drawn off."

This may be compared with the later dramatic version of *Uncle Tom's Cabin*, in which there is a chase across an ice-field which is breaking up. What was used for ice cannot be stated, but the real thing would not be possible.

As the century progressed, the taste for displays of horsemanship developed into a liking for plays involving a military setting, and, if possible, a cavalry skirmish. Such a play was the *Invasion of Russia : an equestrian and military Drama*, first shown here in 1825. These martial entertainments often had whole scenes of action without any dialogue whatever, and into these scenes could be introduced a new and dangerous lure to the public—fire. The following direction is characteristic :

> " He fires his second pistol into a powder barrel, at the same moment that Ismail and the two other officers fire on him. The Citadel is blown up . . . amid the confusion, and in a shower of fire, a general combat on the calcined rocks that surround the Citadel."

The consequences of this fondness for flames were unhappy. Many theatres were burned down during the nineteenth century with great loss of life. Yet there was a ludicrous side to all this, for the Theatre Royal prompt copy of *The Tempest*, which was used in 1839, bears, opposite the printed direction " Enter Ariel " the note " Ball of Fire."

If fire and water were much in demand, because they were exciting, foreign shores were also liked, because they were exotic. *Obi*, an early favourite of the Birmingham audiences, opens thus :—

" A View of an extensive Plantation in Jamaica, the Centre representing Slaves and Oxen in figures tilling the Ground. At the back are Sugar Houses and a practicable Wheel, representing a Mill at work."

This is a typical scene in *The Cabin Boy*, 1864. At the rear of the stage appears the forepart of a ship, which is connected to the quay by a gang-plank. Behind the ship is a sea-scape ; this is a small-scale set by comparison with one in *The Sea*, by C. A. Somerset :—

" Act I, Scene iv . . . A Storm. Part of the Wreck of the Windsor Castle discovered, the Bowsprit extended stiffly, to realise the two beautiful pictures by Dawe— first, a Female struggling, with an Infant in her arms, against the raging Billows ; second, that of a brave Seaman letting himself down from the Bowsprit, and thus suspended between Air and Ocean, snatching both Mother and Infant from a Watery Grave."

Aquatic drama on this scale was apparently a national mania from 1830, when it was popularised by Drury Lane and Sadler's Wells. Later, it came to be satirised. In the

Theatre Royal pantomime for Christmas, 1862, *Puss in Boots*, is the following :—

> " Alas ! The Marquis, my respected master
> Has met with a most terrible disaster,
> Intending, in yon river's glassy flow
> To take a header, a la Boucicault :
> Although no Colleen Bawn was snugly lying
> To be fished up, and nightly saved from dying."

The equestrian drama was back in full strength in 1848. Mazeppa took his wild ride nightly, and the *Fox Hunt* was again revived :

> " The great Popularity which attended the novel Production of the Fox Hunt in London has been equalled by the immense Success . . . in this Town. The exhilarating scenes of the Old English Noble Sport, portraying, with real Fox and Hounds, the Progress of the Fox Chace [*sic*]—the Meet, Break Cover, Leaping the Furze, and the Death of the Fox have been received with Enthusiasm . . . also the beautiful Hanoverian Steed, exemplifying the Death of the Huntsman's Horse, and being carried, on the Shoulders of the Fox Hunters to the Grave. . . . "

Allowance must be made for extravagance, since this is a play-bill advertisement, but the spectacle must, in a barbarous way, have been an exciting one.

Cavalry and flames play a large part in *The Peninsular War*, given in 1851. In the prompt copy which survives, is a finely drawn and coloured sketch of the last set. It represents the interior of a town under siege. On the ramparts is a platform for sentries ; a towered house to the right, belonging to the Governor, has an elaborate fountain outside its gates. The town is attacked and bombarded from the rear of the stage. The wall collapses under fire, at the points marked. There is a cavalry charge through the breach ; the Governor's house is attacked, and the front blown off, to reveal a two-story interior. In the bedroom, a small child is sleeping. The inevitable hero climbs the staircase, now in flames, and rescues the infant. The stairs are by now impassable, so a rope is made from the sheets, and the rescuer descends from the window.

How the Theatre Royal escaped the fate of so many others of the period is a puzzle : but there was only one small fire on the stage, in 1854. The craze for a flaming finale continued, nevertheless, to the end of the century. In *Loyal to the Last*, 1896, the last scene is a struggle in a burning building. The sides fall in, the floor collapses, and the combatants are thrown into a flaming pit, much after the fashion of the *Jew in Malta*, three hundred years earlier.

This theatre did not favour spectacular interiors, though many were complex and colourful ; and some might be called unusual. The fourth act of *The Bondman* takes place in a sulphur mine ; the dramas based on the stories of M. G. Lewis have some vast Gothic interiors ; but the Royal stage manager preferred to spread himself out of doors.

Hazlewood's drama, *The Hop Pickers* (1869), opens thus :

" Extensive Hop Grounds near Wateringbury in Kent, with Drying Houses and the River Medway in the distance . . . (later) . . . View on the Banks of the Thames, near Henley, with the exterior of a Villa."

This is, in a sense, a local scene. The Theatre Royal did not, except in the case of a pantomime, go to such extremes in this direction, as the Prince of Wales Theatre,

which, in 1885, showed a play *Driven from Home*, which
was staged with

> " Magnificent Scenery and Effects in Edgbaston Old
> Church, Raybrook's Mansion near Five Ways, Saint
> Philip's Church and Colmore Row, the Town Hall
> and Council Houses, New Street, the Coach and Horses,
> Worcester Wharf, the Saw Mills (with Machinery in
> action) and Edgbaston Church by Moonlight."

The Royal had, in fact, gone one better than this, for
in 1848 it had exhibited Notre Dame by moonlight. The
slighhtly eerie aways stimulated a Victorian audience, so
the Royal put on crypts, castles, blasted heaths, huge
pieces of Gothic architecture, and dark bridges with black,
evil waters flowing swiftly beneath, ready for the despairing
girl and the inevitable rescue.

MACHINERY AND SETTINGS

The many strange and astonishing plays which were
given at the Theatre Royal during its first century must
have required great ingenuity in those who were responsible
for mounting the productions. How some of the wonders
recounted in play-bills and advertisement were represented
is matter for speculation ; but a large collection of prompt
books, inventories and acting texts gives a fair picture
of the mechanics of the stage.

In all such studies as these, it is well to distrust old
illustrations, from magazines and advertisements, which
show scenes *in situ*, since the artist, in the interests of
effect, often portrayed flats, wings and raking-pieces as
three-dimensional scenery. From lists and cash records,
it is clear that scenery at the beginning of the last century

was not very solid. Mayhew, writing in 1840, says :—

> " There are but three different kinds of scenery . . .
> drops or cloths, flats and set scenes . . . formerly the
> chief part of all stock scenery consisted of drops, as is
> still the case in most country theatres."

If the last remark is correct, the Theatre Royal must
have been unusually well provided with scenery, as the
catalogue of the sale in 1825 will show. Many flats
and set pieces are listed. Later in the century, it became
the practice to hire real articles for use on the stage,
instead of knocking together a property substitute in the
carpenter's shop. It may be remembered, for instance,
that Sheraton furniture was among the goods sold in 1902.

Pictures of sets at the Theatre Royal date from the
early nineteenth century; the first ones are depressing
to look at, as they are usually of a fearful symmetry. This
kind of scene, not unlike the balanced structure of a
Georgian house, is well shown in the first set for
the popular play of *Tom and Gerry*. A symmetrical
table spreads out in front of the audience ; behind it sit
matched rows of guests ; the prompt copy indicates that
the food is matched too ; in the centre is the culinary
keystone, the turkey (the side tables have only fowls) :
behind the bird sits the owner of the hall, and the two
protagonists of the play are disposed on the left and right.
The second scene from the same comedy is just as
balanced, though more elaborate. It shows a ballroom,
with a gallery at the rear of the stage, in which is the
orchestra.

Other kinds of symmetrical setting are shown in
the prompt books, one of which, from *Fortunio*, by
Planché (1843), has a Market Cross as the focal point of

the whole stage : before it, guards and populace are set out with geometrical precision, listening to the herald on the steps of the Cross. The same principle was applied to doors. This illustrates a characteristic nineteenth century device, which was evolved because of the shape of the stage. Theatres of the period had no apron stage, and scarcely a yard of space in front of the curtain. The Theatre Royal was no exception (*see* Plate iv). This picture-frame stage, by its very name, suggests what kind of illusion the actor and dramatist sought—the pictorial. The prompt copies are frequently marked " tableau " ; and this is not merely at the end of a play, when, in any case, a speech to the audience was quite as popular a device, but at the conclusion of acts, scenes—anywhere where the situation made the actors fall into some kind of picturesque group. Often there was a specific intention of reproducing a well-known painting ; the directions in *The Sea*, by Somerset, speak of " realising the two beautiful pictures by Dawe " ; in the scene directions for the play *The Battle of Life*, the stage manager is referred to " the illustrations to Dickens's work," and pages are quoted, though the edition is not ; while a scene in the forest of Bondy, used in the pantomime *Little Red Riding Hood* in 1858, is to be " after the painting by Florio." Nevertheless, some of the authors and managers of the period must have felt hampered by this lack of proscenium room, as do many of their successors to-day, who are still working with theatres put up a century ago, and there were various ways of dealing with the problem. One of these affected the scenery, and it was to have a set with windows or doors at the rear, giving on to a distant prospect, whereby the stage was given the appearance of being deeper than it actually was. Thus, we could look through a room full of dancers, by means of the three doors at the rear of the set, into a room full of card players. In the Throne Room scene of *Fortunio* the gates in the left wing look out on to a prospect of the Grand Square. In another, one window of the room represented looks out to a lane ; the door, to a street. The final development of the idea was achieved by the setting of a house interior. The troublesome fourth wall has been cut away ; over the segmented building, can be seen, on a painted back-cloth, the rest of the village.

This is at the end of the century. One wonders how the elaborate settings of an earlier day were shifted sufficiently quickly to preserve some kind of dramatic illusion. Perhaps this was not aimed at ; the terms in which scenes in a new play were often advertised suggest that the play-goer went to see what new marvel the mechanics had brought forth, and to consider it as a structural triumph, rather than as a part of a dramatic performance. Earlier in this book some details of the state of scene-shifting at the Royal in 1825 have been given. How could such incompetent workmen have made a series of scene-changes in a play where elaborate sets were used for a few moments only ? One way of achieving this is shown by the notes in a prompt copy of *London*. The Prologue to this play is spoken in a scene representing London Bridge in 1703 ; when this ended, the play begins in an entirely different setting. " London Bridge " consisted of two flats run into the third groove in the stage : these could be swiftly slipped out again, and behind them a large part of the next scene was already set. A similar method is used in the play *Scamp o' London* in a scene showing the Birmingham Terminus. The first groove is empty ; in the second are two flats to represent the pillars and gates of the station : groove three bears flats to indicate the offices and other buildings of the station. The great advantage of such an arrangement as this was that a part of the stage could be cut off by a pair of flats, and on this a scene could be erecting while another was being played out in front. The speed and ease of scene-shifting increased as the century progressed and by about 1860, the stage mechanism was almost modern. As early as 1840 it was noted that it was very bad technique to write short scenes, to be played on a limited stage, for the purpose of giving the stage hands time to change a set. The difficulty of working several set scenes continuously was felt nevertheless.

PROPERTIES AND EFFECTS

Properties and effects were perhaps of more importance then than to-day. The latter were regarded in much the same way as certain scenery was—that is, as being very little to do with drama, but as providing an exhibition by itself.

The earliest effects used at the Theatre Royal seem to have been to do with the elements. They were of a spectacular kind. In 1825 was shown a fearful drama called *The Iron Chest*. One scene showed :

" An Ancient Burying-Ground, in which Scene an Hurricane suddenly bursts forth . . . the Thunder Rolls tremendously, and Lightenings glare between the Tombs."

The thunder was created by a machine for which the proprietors paid the large sum of £7, which suggests an apparatus more elaborate than the usual sheet of tin. The lighting effects were probably done by gas, as that had been installed in the buildings for five years.

This was all for spectacle ; for pathos, snow was useful.

In 1825, we are told, " Two snow scenes were exhibited, and deserved the approbation they received."

Snow landscapes were popular, perhaps because they were easy to paint ; they are much in use in *The Waits* of 1849, and *The Peninsular War* of 1851.

The ocean was also much employed for spectacular purposes, as has already been indicated. In 1825 the dramatised version of *The Antiquary* was played, and a stormy sea was let loose. This effect was gained by flooding the stage, and by agitating the water with submarine machinery. A critic acidly remarks : " The machinery for working the water could be seen between each wave," so it must have been crude. Not only the crude, but also the makeshift were common at this time. As the *Theatrical Looker-On* says :—

" Those who are accustomed to the properties of the London theatres can form no idea of the straits to which managers and performers are reduced in ill-appointed country theatres, in an attempt to attain some degree of illusion. Sometimes they are so unblushingly impudent that I have looked with astonishment at the audience who could lend their minds to receive, as the presentation of the person, place or thing actually exhibited to them."

The Birmingham Theatre was a better one than most in the provinces, but it was not very prosperous after the fire of 1820, so that its work often earned censure for being makeshift. A critic, speaking of a revival of an older version of *The Forty Thieves* in 1825,—a critic who had the advantage of knowing all the actors by sight—called the performance

" Humbug. There was not even an ass to carry off the treasure. Shuter stationed himself at the mouth of the robber's cave (which, by the by, looked more like a baker's oven) and chucked the money-bags to Thorne ;

he again pitched them to someone behind the scenes, so that they were flying from one to another like bricks from a cart . . . but the best scene of all was the Oil Jars, in which the thieves were concealed, and of which we were favoured with a sight of four only, videlicet— one *large* one marked ' forty,' faithfully copied from Mr. Lloyd, the tobacconist's shop, and three *little* ones painted on a board. just like the gallipots at a country apothecary's, to fill up a dark corner. However, it shortened Morgiana's labour in the slaughtering way . . . and the execution was very quickly performed (we believe by a small pinch of the thieve's ear) as he ' roared like any sucking dove.' "

The same critic is very shrewd on the subject of stage furniture which was over-worked. There was only " One wretched little table, both for the drawing room and the pig-stye."

In the year when this was written, 1825, there was a sale at the Theatre and the property lists are interesting. Of the more surprising articles, Holyhead Lighthouse, a complete hot-house, clouds and a rack-wheel may be mentioned. These are not so unexpected as certain of the properties of the Theatre Royal, Dublin, however, which, in 1776, had included

" Juliet's Balcony, a small map for Lear, an old toy Gibbet, 11 metal thunder bolts, 67 wooden ditto, 5 stone ditto, 3 baskets for thunder balls, rack in Venice Preserv'd, Elephant in the Enchanted Lady (very bad) and a water fall."

The list bears out the remark by Mayhew, that most of the material used on the provincial stage in the early part of the century was two-dimensional.

It has been said that scenic realism began with the work of Madame Vestris, in 1830. Charles Kean, with his production of *Henry VIII* in 1855, began the archaeological revival. The new interest in having historical settings and costumes which were accurate must have led to an improved state of scenic effect generally. As the century went on, properties became heavier and more genuine. The carpenter became less important when it became possible to hire " the real thing," and what is more, to advertise the makers in the programme. The results were anomalous—a real boat would appear on an artificial sea, for example, with the effect of heightened, rather than diminished artificiality. Special properties began to be mentioned in the press : in the advertisement for *The Queen of Hearts* in 1884, the public is informed that " Queen Victoria's State Carriage " is made " by Mr. J. Rowe." In the days of its prosperity the Royal purchased its period furniture, so that the sale of 1902 included " a fine old Elizabethan buffet, richly carved Louis mahogany drawing-room suite, Jacobean, Sheraton and Chippendale furniture."

The furnishing of the stage became, towards the end of Victoria's reign, like the furnishing of the home—too heavy. There were many stupid little farces played on the stage at that time, which had been written a generation or two earlier. Bowdler's censorship was bad enough—Macready remarked :

" on my way, I read over attentively Bowdler's version of Othello, with which I was not satisfied—unnecessary omissions, and improper passages I thought continued,"

but this was as nothing to the small provincial censor, working in a town full of Nonconformists. The acting copies of the Theatre Royal have whole pages slashed for the sake of a line or two. The censor must have had a very unpleasant mind to see offence in much of what he excised. The effect of this was that scenes in a farce might be cut down to a few lines. It was nevertheless the custom to play these with full furnishing. The stage grew more and more littered up as time went on ; though some lessons had been learned. The artificial balance of the earlier sets vanished. Instead we get scenes like that presented in the first Act of *Loyal to the Last* by T. E. Pemberton. Here the two sides of the scene are in contrast, but not discord, and there is a focal point in the inn-sign, which is off the centre of the stage.

The full weight of the craze for numerous and real properties seems to have fallen on the promoter himself. He was responsible for seeing that articles which actors had to carry on were ready to hand. He had to be prepared with a bunch of real grapes, a written letter from which a character had to read (those to be dramatically burned were treated with turpentine), and, on one occasion, during a performance of *The Cricket on the Hearth* just before the stage direction " cricket heard," the prompter's copy bears the pencilled note " cricket ready." It is likely that the harassed prompter, besides ringing bells for curtains and coloured fires, warning the gas man, keeping in touch with the orchestra and prompting the actors, had also to produce himself the various moans, shouts, babies' cries and other " noises off " noted in his book—even to the chirrupping of the cricket. Realism often went too far, and in the play of *Waterloo* at the frequent direction " cannon heard," the prompter marked his copy " discharge six pistols."

A word may be said about the presentation of the supernatural on the stage of the Theatre Royal. From the early days of the English Theatre, perhaps from the middle ages, when Hell was below stage, and all its evil issues rose to sight, ghosts have been associated with trap doors. The Theatre Royal has always had these : the Agreement for the building of 1774 mentions " Traps." In the sale of 1825, numerous sinking-pieces are mentioned. The floor of the stage was constantly required to collapse— struggling men vanished through the flaming boards, fugitives took refuge in cellars, and, on one occasion, a complete working fountain sank through the stage, in an enthralling manner. Many full-scale plays have a require- ment noted in the scenic directions as " Practical Trap." The odd thing about the Theatre Royal, in this matter, is that, in spite of these traps, it preferred to introduce its ghosts in another manner. Spirits of the departed usually swept across the rear of the stage, or rose from the back and ascended towards Heaven, casting looks of sorrow or joy on the earthly actors. It is clear that many of these spectres were artificial figures, and not played by some solid super in the cellarage. The stage directions are an indication of this, thus :—

" The Shade of Gilbert appears, it turns, and is worked over gradually to her."

The most popular play of the supernatural was *The Dead Guest* and in this the spectre did not rise from below stage, but entered from the wings, as the illusion of ghostliness was captured by the apparatus known and advertised, as " Professor Pepper's Ghost." This came to Birmingham in 1863 ; and while it was playing the full rights of the invention were vested in Simpson, the manager of the Royal.

COSTUME

The Theatre Royal was built at a time when there was a new interest in antiquarianism—an interest which was associated with the beginnings of the Romantic Movement. The results, in the theatre, were seen in the costume and scenery; there was now some attempt to make these historically accurate. Previously, from the time of the Restoration, the first requirement in the costume of the serious stage had been richness. There were also certain conventional items of dress, such as trains for tragic heroines, and plumes for heroes. Garrick had started a fashion for having genuine wealth on the stage—real velvets and jewels. There was, however, no attempt at portraying the correct costume of a period, or even of a country, as is proved by such pictures as those of Garrick as Macbeth.

Birmingham had witnessed a performance in correct dress as early as 1747, when *The Siege of Damascus* was played at the theatre in Moor Street. It was announced that " All the Characters in the Play will be dressed in the proper Habits, as the Greeks and Romans then appeared."

The advertisement indicates that such a thing was rare, and at the Theatre Royal the old customs lasted long :—

" It was long possible to witness a performance of one of Shakespeare's historical plays in the court costume of the eighteenth century."

Realistic costume was thus usually announced as a part of the evening's attraction. A pantomime of 1796 was clad

" In new Dresses, after the Manner of the Catabaws, with a War Hoop, Preparations for Battle, and an Extraordinary Method of Lying in Ambush."

A pantomime dress for Captain Cook was valued at £40,

which suggests opulence ; so, too, do certain articles in the sale of 1825. For example :

> " Black velvet Shape, trimmed with Gold and lined, with straps, Jacket and Cloak £4 10 0
> Various scarlet Hussar Dresses ..... £4 0 0 each.
> Admiral's Dress, complete .... £10 0 0 "

On the other hand, much of the material was very shoddy, and in poor condition.

Two years before this sale Kemble put on his famous production of *King John* in London, which started the series of elaborate archaeological revivals for which the century is known. The costume for the play was devised by the antiquarian and playwright, Planché, and it caused a new interest in historical pageantry which affected not only production, but the drama that was being written.

In general, the Theatre Royal did not imitate the London splendour. Classical tragedy, in which the age was so unhappily rich, was played in rather vague robes. The directions at the beginning of *The Distress'd Mother*, a translation of Racine's *Andromache*, in the edition of 1819 used at the theatre, illustrates the general lines—

> " *Pyrrhus*—Buff and silver Cuirass, and Lambrakeens, purple velvet Robe, richly embroidered, white Shirt, spangled, flesh arms and legs, and Sandels.
> *Orestes*—white kerseymere Robe, Shirt and Belt embroidered . . . and Bandeau.
> *Pylades*—white Shirt, spangled, scarlet Robe and Belt embroidered, flesh arms &c.
> *Andromache*—black muslin Petticoat, Tunic and Robe trimmed with black Fringe. Second Dress, white muslin Petticoat, Tunic and Robe trimmed with Silver. Tiara of Jewels on the Head.
> *Hermione*—white china crepe Dress, and Drapery trimmed with Gold. Tiara for the Head.
> *Cleone*—white muslin Dress."

Spectacular historical productions were not favoured, perhaps because of expense. *Measure for Measure* was played in 1883 "with all the original armour &c," but a hard-worked provincial wardrobe would have little room for elaborate costumes. Even essentials of dress and dress-properties were not always in good repair. Macready in 1849, records an experience at Birmingham :

> " Acted Hamlet under very distressing circumstances, a dress not fitting me . . . a sword every minute sticking in my shoes, and breaking in my hand when trying to use it."

Perhaps the attitude of the Theatre Royal towards historical plays may be best expressed by the directions to *The Tower of London*, which suggest, for the dress, " select ad libitum from any Play of the Elizabethan Age ; or earlier, say Richard III."

Similarly, the style of a later generation can be summed up in a quotation from the sale in 1902 :—

> " 30 seaweed dresses, 24 velvet combinations, a Newmarket coat, silk lined, as used by Miss Vesta Tilley. Six dresses, as worn by six of Birmingham's handsomest girls, when Miss Vesta Tilley sang the well-known song, ' Oh, you girls ! ' all embroidered silk and velvet, by Worth, of Paris."

LIGHTING

In 1763, Covent Garden was lit from the back by six groups of twelve candles. Garrick used concealed lamps and footlights. By 1774, when the Theatre Royal was built, drama was a pictorial art rather than a rhetorical one. This was the direct result of the shape of the stage, and the methods of lighting. On an Elizabethan apron stage, under the summer sky, a completely different style of acting had been required. The mere fact of drama having gone indoors must have had a great effect. In thinking of the indoor theatre, we must disabuse our minds completely of the modern arrangement of lights— a dark auditorium, a row of foot-lights and a box in the rear of the spectators, projecting rays of varying colour and intensity on to the stage. In the Theatre Royal, as in other theatres of the period, lighting came from on the stage, and frequently from behind the stage ; and the auditorium would have chandeliers lit throughout the performance.

Until 1809, the theatre was lit by tallow candles. On special occasions, such as its first opening in 1774, and after the reconstruction in 1792, wax was used. Tallow is smoky and smelly. In 1809, the proprietors found the old candles a false economy. The theatre was lit by " Spermaceti Oil, and Spermaceti or Wax Candles, that used at present being considered injurious to the Painting." Patent lamps were fitted over the Stage Boxes.

In those days, lighting effects on the stage must have been limited, and, though a pantomime of 1800 had a scene showing " the Garden of the Sylph, brilliantly illuminated," there was little remarkable in this sphere until the introduction of gas. Birmingham was the home of the pioneers of gas-lighting, and one of them, Matthew Boulton, of the Boulton and Watt works, Soho, was on the Theatre Royal Committee. The theatre was rebuilt in 1820, and gas was introduced from the new main in the street outside. It seems likely that it was first used in the auditorium only, for, in the next year there are notes of repairs to chandeliers. In a few years there were border-lights, footlights, floats (*i.e.*, lights suspended over the stage), and some used for special effects, such as illuminating particular actors ; these last were usually operated from the rear of the stage. Spectacular lighting effects may be dated from Macready's production of *King Lear* in London, 1838, when gas was used for the storm scenes with lurid results. The usual method of intensifying the light was by means of a lime block, which, becoming incandescent, gave off a very brilliant white radiance, and, it should be added, a great deal of heat. Screens of tinted glass or other materials were used for colour effects.

The following practices seem to have been customary at the Theatre Royal in the era of the lime-light ; they are deduced principally from the notes in prompt copies as the prompter was responsible for keeping in touch with the man in charge of the illuminations. The curtain would rise on a brilliantly-lit stage, about which a few characters would be moving ; there would be no speech for a moment. Then the first speaking actor would enter and the lights were dimmed for him. The crepuscular effect would have its emotional result in the auditorium, and would attract attention to the actor in a sufficiently subtle way. Dim lighting was also found useful in romantic passages, so that the love-scenes in *The Widow of Marmentiers* were played with the lights half down. A similar device was in use for ghostly scenes when the gas was turned low, and it was soon discovered that certain colours have a chilling effect on an audience.

There are no early examples of the modern pantomime usage of illuminating the villain with green, nevertheless, it is a colour whose effects were known. In *The Prophet*, in 1850, it was used considerably. A camp fire scene at night is thus lit :—" green mediums to side lights, others all down." A faint green light here would intensify the eerie darkness round the fire. In the same play, green is the sole lighting used for a dungeon scene. More elaborate use of colour is to be found in the last decade of the century, in a prompt copy of *Ben My Chree*. For the opening scenes, white limelights, some from the rear of the stage, were used. Scenes in sunlight, or interiors with lamps were flooded with amber. Individual actors were picked out in white, and fighting took place in a pool of angry red.

These methods are to be found in the much earlier text of *One o'Clock*, a ghostly drama by Matthew Gregory Lewis, where there are numerous lighting directions, as " Attend to lights and changing colour of the Moon . . . red Gauze to Moon . . . black Veil to Moon."

The moon has been a favourite subject for the lighting experimenter, as moonlight has a special emotional value. In *Boyne Waters* shown in fig. xvii, there is a bedroom window which is marked in the prompter's sketch, " window for Moon to shine through." This suggests that its main purpose was for the lighting effect, which would, of course, be secured from the rear of the stage. In *L'Assomoir*, which appeared under various titles, the lighting seems to have been almost entirely from the back. The stage was flooded with limelight through windows in the back of the set. In *The Dead Guest*, in 1863, a kind of spot-lighting from back stage was introduced : the direction reads : " the rays of the moon falling on the floating body of Basta."

The most effective lighting device, in an artificially lit house is, paradoxically, always the absence of lights, and darkness was often well exploited. An illustration to *Jack Sheppard* shows two figures struggling in a gloomy stair-well, and brandishing torches, which appear to be the only source of light. In the melodrama *The Drunkard's Children*, in 1856, a midnight scene was played in a stage darkened as far as the requirements of the actors would allow. In *London* two scenes—one in a loft where a fugitive takes refuge—were played with lights turned right down. Lanterns were introduced in the second scene. This particular play used the amusing convention which still persists—that when one or two small, visible lights on the stage are removed, it becomes instantly very dark. Some candles are taken from a room, and all stage lighting is at once turned half down.

Gas had several serious disadvantages. It was not so easy to control as electricity now is. It was likely to hiss loudly, especially when used in a lime-light apparatus. The heat of the auditorium would be much increased; while the actors on whom it was directed, and the orchestra, which sat next to it, would suffer great discomfort from the radiation.

The greatest problem of all was the danger from fire. The Theatre Royal had been twice burned out, so the precautions were unusually elaborate. There were even water-taps on the stage, as a safeguard against the incendiary plays of the period. By 1885, however, the footlights were all electric, operating from a generating machine inside the house, and, in 1896, power was introduced from outside.

CHAPTER V

THE PERFORMANCE

ACTING

Any study of the style and quality of acting at the Theatre Royal is bound to be of a rather speculative kind.   Dramatic critics are capricious folk.   Those of the nineteenth century were often persons of vulgar taste, and may not be relied upon to give a true and useful account of the performances they saw.   Most of them, like one or two present day book reviewers, are more concerned with their own jokes than the work of the actors.

Personal reminiscences by people who saw Irving and his contemporaries are apt to be clouded by the fact of the reporter's age, both at the time of telling, and at the time when he saw the actor.   There is also a tradition that the acting of Irving—or Bernhardt, or Garrick, or Burbage, was such as will never be seen again.   Nevertheless, Birmingham has had a good number of dramatic journals, especially in the 1820's, from which a picture can be built up of the acting standards of the day.

The Theatre Royal was closely associated, from its early days, with two of the most famous actors of the time—Macready and Mrs. Siddons.   Macready made his first stage appearance at the Royal in 1810, and was always a favourite there.   He was noted for restraint in his acting. So too was Mrs. Siddons, who, it is said, purchased a bust

of herself in a Birmingham shop, which was so unlike her
that the seller did not recognise her.

This led her to take up the study of sculpture, from which
she learned that the secret of effective appearance on the
stage lay in line rather than gesture. She therefore
reduced her gestures on the stage to the simplest, using no
action that was redundant. In the eighteenth century,
when she was acting at the Royal, performances were of a
good standard. M'Cready, the manager, used to go up to
London and pick a fine cast to bring to Birmingham in the
summer. His season was a short one of three months or so,
and the company did not grow stale. When he gave up
his connection with the London stage, he began to collect
a stock company, many of them wandering players, who,
temporarily engaged, stayed on taking odd parts and making
the financing of the Theatre difficult. The effect on the
standard of performance was also deleterious. A critic
of 1825 is making a constant plea for dignity among the
actors, and for a reduction of cheap, needless gesture :—

" His action, which as a boy was graceful, is now the
reverse, and consists of one unvaried motion like the
sails of a windmill—up and down."

The stock actor, Matthews, receives the comment :—

" Would he express the signs of woe
He slaps his breast and points his toe ;
If agony's to be expressed,
He points his toe, and slaps his breast."

Another critic says, of Mude :—

" He has a provincialism of pronouncing now and
then his u's like oo's . . . his right hand often assumes
the appearance of a finger post."

This comment on pronunciation is interesting. It
seems as if actors developed a style of their own, like

Irving's " Gud " for " God," and " me " for " my."   So, for example, " Archer, a disciple of the Kemble school . . . fill all thy bones with AITCHES."

This form of speech was affected by the oncoming tide of realism ; but diction must have been very stilted throughout the century. It is only necessary to consider the things which actors were required to say ; for instance, this is in the mouth of a woman in Howard's *Monte Cristo* :

> " I no longer seek instruction in war and politics ; therefore I pray that you will spare me the bellicose discussion."

This is one example of many. Characters from high life were required to speak in a highly artificial diction, which raises the possibility of their having uttered a kind of fashionable speech used by some of the aristocracy in reality. The delivery of such lines could not, however, have been realistic, because the basis of the speech is artificial. Moreover, in the first half of the nineteenth century, it was considered ludicrous for actors to make themselves at ease on the stage—Macready and Dickens were astonished and outraged at a French performance in which the characters sat down whenever the time seemed appropriate. They were accused of treating the play with levity.

Unnatural stance and action may very well have been the accepted thing in view of the artificial nature of the grouping of scenery and actors. Ceremonial was a popular device, and any scene with a large number of people in it seems to have been preferred to a dialogue. The curtain would commonly rise on a carefully arranged crowd scene—*Fortunio*, Act I is a good example. The sketch in the prompt book shows an absolutely symmetrical crowd. At the other end of the play was the heart-rending death group.

This was always carefully balanced : the dying man was set in the middle of the stage, supported by one of the chief female characters ; most of the remainder of the cast was arranged round these two in equal groups. Perhaps the most blatant examples of this usage are the last scenes of *Enoch Arden* and *Ravenscroft*.

A dead man often died wordless, with some touching or significant action. There was quite a tradition of mimed endings : and openings too. The most extended example of this among the Theatre Royal plays is the first scene of *Nobody's Child*, by W. Phillips :

> " Two sailors discovered at table . . . they knock oᴌ the table for a drink . . . potboy comes out of the inn to serve them . . . village lass comes from dairy with pitchers of milk, and passes off . . . page comes on with letters, posts them in the Post Office, and passes off . . . milkman enters dairy with milk and yoke, boy enters with jug, he is served, business, milkman exits, boy exits, then sneaks into the dairy . . . dairymaid enters from dairy with basket of eggs and butter, and exit . . . John Pornic enters, goes to Post Office, receives letters, shows joy and exit . . . enter Pedlar, shows and sells his wares, business and exit . . . Sailors exeunt when Pedlar comes on . . . all off before Lucy enters . . . enter Miss Lucy Tregarvon, wearing riding boots. . . . as she comes down the stage, Patty Lavrock heard singing off stage."

The first words of the play are then spoken.

At the end of a light play, farce or romantic drama, the cast might line up, and, without any dramatic pretence, come forward, one by one, to speak to the audience in the age-old plea for favour. Sometimes one actress would speak in the manner of the Prologue of other days, sometimes all would have a line or two, perhaps in verse.

The audience was also addressed almost directly in

certain situations in the play. As now, the clown of pantomime might confide over the footlights, and the villain
frequently addressed his fumings to the Pit. The reason
for this was bad dramatic technique in the playwright—the
actor often being under the necessity of explaining his
actions, because otherwise no one could have guessed
what it was that motivated them. Formal soliloquies were
always addressed to the auditorium. To speak one in a
natural manner was so unusual as to call for comment. A
critic is pleased and surprised to see Bunn, in 1825, giving
the " dagger " speech in *Macbeth* not to the Pit, but facing
the side door to which the dagger was supposed to lead
him.

The actor who pleased was rewarded by applause in the
middle of the scene, which was the signal, sometimes, for
him to repeat whatever had caught the public fancy—the
speech, usually—just like an operatic aria. Other actors
on the stage might applaud as well. On the other hand,
bad acting called forth thunder from the Gods. It was
not unknown for an unpopular actor to be driven off the
stage by execrations. At the Royal one night, an actor
missed his cue, and, being hissed, " the wrong actor took
the hiss to be for him, and stood frowning and knitting
his brows quite tragically."

The audience, however, more naive than to-day, was
prepared to accept the accidents which befell a small stock
company :

> " The first thing we heard before the curtain rose
> was that the principal part of Barbaya was to be read by
> Mr. Webster, for Bennet. It was vastly funny to see
> Webster slapping his breast, and flourishing with one
> hand, while he held his book in the other."

This, incidentally, is a picture of the flamboyant school of acting. The stock company was worked very hard indeed, and things like this were not uncommon :

" The stage door suddenly opened (in the middle of the performance) and out bounced Mr. Bennet. He proceeded immediately to justify himself by stating that he had applied for the book with his part ferquently, and that it was as frequently refused him, and that he did not obtain it until Wednesday morning, when it was too late to study it."

If Kean, or some other London celebrity, came down for a week, he might give five Shakespearian plays, or their equivalent. The stock company had to be ready to support him in these—and when a favourite was playing, the curtain might not fall until two in the morning. Either, therefore, there was no sleep, or no rehearsal. The supporting of the Royal Companies was not always good. Macready complained, in 1841,

" Acted Macbeth with great spirit, and was marred, utterly deprived of my effects by the ' support " of a Mr. —— and others in the last Act. . . . I tried to act Richelieu, and did my best with a company and a Mr. —— that would paralyse a Hercules. The house was enormous. I went forward to a call I could not evade . . . acted Cardinal Richelieu as well as the wretched murdering of the other characters would let me."

The period was one of change, and definite statements about its acting would be unsafe. Realism began with " Society," in 1865, and acting then changed its basis. It seems that the cheap drama of the age continued to be cheaply acted.

MUSIC

Music and drama have always been companions. The Puritans thought all musicians were godless, and expelled them from the society of decent men, but at the Restoration, the fiddlers, poor and ragged, joined with the players, and founded theatre orchestras. At the end of a piece, they would appear on the stage and play a dance, in which the whole audience might join, after the fashion of the end of a masque.

It is not surprising, then, to find that the Theatre Royal had musical associations from its foundation. In the days when it was unlicensed, the programme ostensibly consisted of a concert, after which a play might be given free, by the actors. When the house became licensed, this concert persisted in the form of a " musical after-piece." Under Macready, these were allowed to decline, so that when Elliston, who was apparently a man of musical taste, made on offer for the Theatre, a correspondent hoped that he would restore " the Musical After-Pieces, neglected these four years by Macready, who has no ear for Music."

At this time the theatre orchestra would be hard worked. Programmes always included several songs and dances, which would require accompaniment. Music was played before the curtain rose—receiving, perhaps, even less attention than it does now—and many of the effects were provided by the orchestra.

The first reference to the use of music in direct connection with the action of a play at the Theatre Royal is in a prompt book of the pantomime of *Harlequin Mariner* of 1816 ; for the entry of the first character, there were " eight bars of introductory music." The practice of thus announcing an entry has persisted to-day, and has been borrowed by the film, and elaborated into the *Leit-motif* of music-drama. The old style is laughed at now : but when, in the play *The Streets of New York* given in 1864, the protagonist appeared, and the prompter signalled to the orchestra to play *Here the Conquering Hero Comes* the audience was just as stirred as is the modern cinema-goer by the constant symphonic undercurrent to every scene of emotion on the screen.

Music was used to cover the long silent openings, especially in the pantomimes, where no word would be spoken for several minutes after the curtain rose. Before the entry of an important character, the orchestra's job would be to increase tension in the audience—so, for example, it begins to play a little before the quite unexpected entry of the fugitive in *London*. When the immortals spoke, in pantomimes, solemn strains accompanied them. In the " Transformations " and in the emotional moments of the melodrama the orchestra played a " strong chord." It provided appropriate music for storms—a gong was almost always introduced here—and attended to sundry effects, such as the striking of clocks.

In the critical writings of the *Looker-On* there are some observations on the vocal music of the theatre, for instance :

" We shall take pleasure in commending even the Chorus Singers, when they wash their faces and sing in tune."

But the chief concern of the writer is the effect of foreign music. First of all, he does not like such music :

" We dislike to hear chambermaids warbling bravuras, or sailors chanting Italian airs . . . Rossini has fairly routed Doctor Arne."

He then speaks of the effects of this taste, which was apparently a popular one. " Simple English songs done up in bravura fashion," were ridiculous enough, but the use of this style had a bad dramatic effect too :—

" What would the Immortal Bard think, were it permitted to revisit the Earth, and find the melancholy, sentimental Olivia singing sprightly songs, and wandering in all luxuriance of scientific cadenza with Viola " ?

The critic is, however, pleased by the good music to a bad *Macbeth*, and, speaking of *The Comedy of Errors*, he says :

"this play is only fit for the closet . . . and was only rendered bearable by the introduction of the beautiful music."

The actor was required to be able to sing, it seems. Was the result good ? A journal of 1827 suggests that Birmingham had a high musical taste : " Birmingham is a very musical town, and none are better judges. Sir Richard, you must keep up to the mark." Macready recalls how, as a child in 1808 he saw the house packed to hear the singer, Mrs. Billington :

" For a week, the Theatre was every night crowded . . . to suffocation, but I can only recall the figure of a very lusty woman, and the excitement of the audience."

On the other hand, musical taste in the nineteenth century was very poor. To-day, the public at large, in spite of a liking for a few hackneyed pieces by the romantic composers, which are usually wrongly known as " classical," has clearly an execrable taste in music. At the same time there are English composers who are writing works of a real musical value. In the Early Victorian age, scarcely anyone in England could be called a real composer of music. Not only was the taste of the ordinary household exemplified by pieces of the kind to be found in the " Star Folio " series, but the " major composers " of the time were mostly facile or pompous.

In 1825 Paganini gave a recital at the Theatre Royal. He was not a man limited to a particular class of violin music, but a master who could play anything,—not a virtuoso of the type of Sydney Smith, the pianist, who had great dexterity of musical execution but no taste whatever. If the accounts of his personality are true, he was not the sort of man to be bullied into playing this or that kind of work by a Theatre Manager. The only thing which would condition his choice of programme was the kind of audience to which he was playing. At the Theatre Royal, having been vulgarly announced as " the one-string violinist," he gave, between two farces, a thoroughly poor programme, of works clearly intended to impress by their cheap brilliance and no more. This does not argue a very high level of musical appreciation in the audience. Nor can the new fragments of manuscript music used by the orchestra which survive do anything to alter the picture. Theatrical music was often as cheap then as music hall pieces are to-day.

It was the custom—and still is in the pantomime—to introduce popular songs into the evening's entertainment. The Christmas Pantomime had long contained well-known airs, though usually with words written specially, but about 1860, songs with choruses were first used, in which the audience could join. There was no attempt at realism in the introduction of a song : the character simply stepped forward and began. They were usually of a comic nature, and sung to a well-known tune, without any special setting. At times, airs were taken from opera, and given as individual entertainment, with a part of the programme to themselves. This is probably what is meant by such notes as " Fra Diavolo songs, and A Stray Parrot " in Littlehale's Diary. Full operas were sometimes given by visiting companies.

Later in the nineteenth century it was a regular practice to have a brass band of local or military repute to give a " Selection " during the evening. The programme was of the kind which can still be heard in the parks of provincial towns on a Sunday afternoon. Musical effects became more and more formidable, perhaps because the melodrama was growing highly emotional in the hands of writers who had not the skill to convey and create emotion without the use of mechanical, scenic and musical aids. The development was widespread. In 1885 a Birmingham commentator is much impressed by the musical arrangements for a London production :—

" A new peal of bells is being cast for the Lyceum Faust. A new organ will be a feature of the Cathedral Scene, and the Walpurgis Night Revels will be under the control of a famous continental Ballet Master."

One other feature of the music of the Theatre Royal must be mentioned, though, as it has nothing to do with the regular programme, and has been fully dealt with by another writer, it can only be dealt with briefly here. The Birmingham Hospital held a number of shares in the Theatre, from a very early time, and usually had a representative on the Committee. For many years, by arrangement with the proprietors, the Music Festivals, whose object was the raising of money for the Hospital, were held in the buildings of the Theatre Royal.

CHAPTER VI

PANTOMIME

HOWEVER valid the claim may be that the origin of pantomime is to be found in the comedies of ancient Greece, the immediate source of English mime was the Italian *Commedia dell' Arte*. This was not strictly mimic, since there was some dialogue, but the chief part of this entertainment was a series of dances, of a formal pattern by stock characters. The comedy was of two kinds—the Extemporal Masque, and the Lazzi. The first has a descriptive name; the second was a more boisterous form of amusement. Italian comedy soon became overloaded with formal characters, but when the play came to France it was much simplified so that there were only four actors—Pantaloon, Clown, Harlequin and Columbine. The story was of young love outwitting the opposition of senile fatherhood. Harlequin was the lover of Pantaloon's daughter, Columbine. The old father was opposed to the match, so Harlequin enlisted the help of the servant, Clown. A series of amusing adventures followed, in which Pantaloon chased the couple, and was frequently tricked and abused. The lovers were finally united.

The situations of this comedy, and the posturings of Harlequin were all formal. Harlequin was the main character, which is why, long after he ceased to be more than a mere dancer in a short episode at the end of a nineteenth century pantomime, his name still appeared in a sub-title on the play-bill. His dances were all significant, like the actions of a ballet dancer. As Rich says :

" A common Lazzaroni, when shown one of these compositions will at once explain the purpose of the action, which a scholar, with all his learning, cannot divine."

This character came from France to England in the seventeenth century. The *Commedia dell'Arte* had been known to the Elizabethans, and the Privy Council, in 1573, asked the Lord Mayor to permit " liberty " to certain Italian players. Thomas Heywood speaks of " Pantaloons, Harlakeans, in which the French, but especially the Italians, have been excelling in this country."

Nevertheless, the full performance never came here : the reason may have been the character who is not mentioned—Columbine. The part would have to be played by a woman, and the Elizabethans would not have actresses on their stage. Harlequin, however, is well-known. In 1607 Day wrote *The Travels of Three Brothers*. In this, the comedian Kempe had a part, and, during the action an Italian Harlequin was announced, performed his dances and attitudes, and was assisted by Kempe. An Italian Harlequin also played before Charles I in 1637, while Mrs. Aphra Ben introduced characters in the roles of Harlequin and Scaramouche into a play, *The Emperor of the Moon*, in 1687.

The first person to attempt an English pantomime was Rich. From 1717 to 1760 he staged plays in the form of a classical or mythological fable, between each act of which was given an episode in the courtship of Harlequin and his lady. These were of a strictly conventional style and without dialogue. Rich himself took the role of Harlequin, and made it the main part of the play, as it had been abroad. As time went on the fable and the episodes gradually became separated, the one developing into an " Opening " and the other into a subsequent " Harlequinade." Soon they ceased to have any unity, so that the result is the extraordinary convention, which persisted until the middle of the next century, of a pantomime being two distinct plays, the second being only connected with the first in so far as the main characters of the Opening were supposed to be transformed into the figures of the Harlequinade.

Rich was followed by Grimaldi. He first appeared in pantomime in 1739. His part was that of Clown, which he extended until it was the main role of the Harlequinade. He added his own native wit to the formal humour of the part, and was so successful and popular that his Christian name has been given to all clowns since. Pantaloon became his butt, and the lovers degenerated to a pair of dancers, though Harlequin still had the most spectacular action of the play—his leap.

At one point in the chase he was expected to make a leap through the face of a clock, and there are many tales about this dangerous feat—how actors were severely injured by the clumsiness of the super whose business it was to catch the flying figure.

The form was still mimic, but Grimaldi introduced songs and choruses. One of them, *Hot Codlins*, was for long a favourite. The audience delighted to supply the last line of each verse, which was of a slightly improper kind—and here we may find the origin of the modern practice of " joining in the chorus." Besides this song, Grimaldi introduced the simple devices which became traditional in the clowning trade—the red-hot poker, the sausages and the buttered slide. He retired in 1828, worn out and pathetic, but it was his great clowning ability which had maintained the importance of the Harlequinade.

After Grimaldi, the opening episode became longer and longer. At this period the Extravaganza was very popular, and this form of comic entertainment, whose chief exponent was Planché, had a considerable effect on the final form of pantomime, and encouraged the development of the Opening. Planché wrote a full " speaking pantomime " in 1818, *Little Red Riding Hood*. It was not a success. Another " speaking opening " was presented at Covent Garden in 1830, by Peake. Again it was unpopular. There was no further attempt until Mark Lemon wrote a pantomime, based on the old form, for Madame Celeste, who presented it at the Adelphi in 1857. From this time dates the style of pantomime known to the Victorians—an elaborate presentation of a known story, humorous and musical in treatment. This was followed by a shorter exhibition of dancing, based on the old story of the lovers, and given by a little troupe of professionals. In the end, even this fell into disuse, and the Harlequinade, the very origin of pantomime, is known no more. The artists of the music hall came to play in pantomime, bringing their tricks with them ; the Clown became eclipsed by them, his elementary humour paled beside their rapid dialogue. The chorus of ample flesh and voice came, too, from the same source. The season was recognised ; it expanded, until it now often runs from Christmas until April. The play has become a treat for children. Much of its former humour and skill is lost, because the early pantomimes were played by professional actors, whereas now dancing and singing ability and good looks are more important. There has, however, been a recent tendency to use well-known screen actresses in the leading parts. The motive is presumably one of publicity. But these experiments have been encouraging for most of the actresses have had experience of the stage, and have given a new life to old characters. People have been lamenting the decay of pantomime for a hundred years which is, perhaps, rather pointless. Planché says regretfully : " There was once as regular a plot as might be found in melodrama."

What is much more worthy of attention is the amazing metamorphosis of the form.

In the collection of manuscript and printed plays of the Theatre Royal, made principally by M. H. Simpson during the nineteenth century, there is an abundance of pantomime material. Most of it is to do with Christmas pantomime, an entertainment introduced here by the elder Simpson in the winter of 1840–41. There are some rough and almost illegible manuscripts, many only fragmentary, of earlier openings, but they are of little service. They usually represent some local shop—a butcher was favoured, as this gave plenty of scope for the use of the comic sausages—and the duping either of tradesman or buyer. The humour is rather crude, consisting of a character's getting his head stuck in a bottle, and of beatings and trippings, but a lively actor with a genius for drollery might make something very amusing of the situations.

The first full pantomime of which the entire text is extant was written specially for the Theatre Royal in 1805, by a Mr. Cherry. Its title is *The Magic of British Liberty, or, the Disgregation of Napoleon . . . a National Pantomime.* It was played during the Napoleonic wars, and was published, price sixpence, in the hope of stimulating public morale.

There is, however, a much earlier source of information

than this. A pantomime called *Harlequin Mariner* was given in 1796. It proved to be very popular, and on the back of a play bill for the 12th of August in that year, appeared the following announcement :—

" The Manager having been requested to adopt the London Mode of presenting the Public with a Narrative of the Plot, Scenery, Machinery &c of the Pantomime . . . in Compliance with such Application, he herewith gives an Abstract of HARLEQUIN MARINER, or the Fairy of the Oak. Performed with general Approbation, and announced for Representation this Evening."

There follows a detailed account of the performance, which is of sufficient interest to be quoted in full :

Scene I :—

Tempestuous Sea, Ship in Distress, violent Storm, Rain and Lightning : the Vessel goes to the Bottom, and one of the Crew clings to a Mast, by Aid of which he gets on Shore, is going to hang himself on the withered Branch of an old Oak, which breaks, the Trunk opens, and a Fairy appears, converts the melancholy Sailor into gay fantastic Harlequin, who receives his magical Sword from the Animated Serpent which traverses the Stage, and is generally allowed to be a very ingenious Piece of Mechanism.

Scene II :—

A Village—Pantaloon and Columbine conducted home by the Clown. He refuses Admittance to Harlequin, who, by Magic, suspends him in the Air—on his Exclamations Watchmen come to strike Harlequin ; he waves his Sword, and their Lanthorns and Poles ascend to the Clouds. The Lover and his servant appear, and are received with Extacy by Pantaloon : he sends for a Lawyer to draw up the Marriage Articles : as he is following the old Gentleman, Harlequin gets into his Gown, Wig &c., and the Lawyer disappears ; In his Disguise he enters the House, is perceived, and makes his Escape up through the Ceiling, in a most astonishing Manner ; the Clown is left with a Candle burning, which alternately changes to three Candles, and from three to one. Harlequin is pursued by Pantaloon, and jumps over ten Men, forward and backward :—they seize him, put him into a Sack, and when they think he is surely there, they find his Dress only.

Scene : [*sic*]—

A country Ale House, the Sign of the Bull and Punch Bowl :—Harlequin's Flight with Columbine, on Horseback pursued by Lover, Pantaloon and Clown, whose Horse throws him.

As he is getting Refreshment, a Waggoner comes and calls for Drink, makes Acquaintance with the Clown. Harlequin cuts off the Waggoner's Head, sets it on a Table—the Head, in the most wonderful and incredible manner. Smoaks, Drinks &c. . . . The Punch Bowl changes to a Dog, he attacks the Bull and is thrown by him ; Columbine is brought Home by her Father and Lover ; Harlequin gets into the House concealed in a Hamper, and escapes with Columbine. Clown goes to drink, and is, in sight of the Audience, encreased to a most enormous Size. Harlequin and Columbine, much fatigued, in a Garden, where Orange Trees appear in Blossom ;—by seeming Magic, Harlequin makes the Fruit appear, and Columbine is refreshed. Father again takes Columbine, leaves her at Home, and pursues Harlequin, who takes Shelter in a Dog Kennel, where being perceived, he instantly changes it to an elevated Pigeon House, and from that to a Prison, in which the Lover and Pantaloon are confined. Harlequin takes the Advantage, and with Columbine goes to an Ordinary to regale : he is pursued, jumps through a Window, and leaves all in confusion, having occasioned " a great Clatter among the Moveables." Columbine, for obstinacy, is thrown into the Cavern of Vice. from which she is conveyed, by the Power of Enchantment, to the most magnificent Scene that Imagination can fancy—the

Temple of Virtue, where Hymen unites her with Harlequin, and the Piece ends with a Dance, and a most admirable Group, representing Cupid and the Loves."

Similarly, on July 23rd, 1795, after *Othello* and a song :—
" will be added a Pantomime Entertainment, called Magic and Mirth, or Harlequin Restoration . . . in the Course of the Pantomime will be introduced the following Incidents—Harlequin's Animation and Original Attitudes, Gladiator's Scene, Sedan Chair, the celebrated Moving Figure, and Harlequin's Flight across the Stage. The whole to conclude with a new Rural Scene, painted by Mr. Banks, and a Dance."

On the 10th of August that year was shown :—

" a new Pantomime . . . called Harlequin Negro, or Revels in the Indies. In the Course of the Pantomime will be introduced the Scene of a Distant Country, a Wash House, and Hay Stack . . . to conclude with a Dance and a Grand View of the British Fleet riding at Anchor."

It may be seen at once that the subjects of these pantomimes are not those used at the present time. *Blue Beard* was shown in 1796, but the other stories, such as *Babes in the Wood*, which is as old as 1594, and the tales of *Cinderella* and *Beauty and the Beast* are not yet used. Next it can be seen that these entertainments were on a large scale. It is clear the *Harlequin Mariner*, for example, needed a great deal of scenery, stage effects and trick mechanics. The chief aim is to pander to the love of spectacle which the playgoers of the Theatre Royal always seem to have had. Thus, things are introduced which are quite extraneous to the original Harlequin story,—Rural Scenes, and the British Fleet.

Birmingham has had a long reputation for good pantomime, the beginnings of which can be seen here, when anything as elaborate as this would be scarcely known

outside London. In connection with this elaboration, the
increasing number of characters may be noticed. The
cast of *Harlequin's Restoration*, besides the traditional figures
of the Harlequinade, included Mother Shipton, Sir
Amorous Vain, Rooney O'Gaffey, Miss Frill (with a Welch
Song), Miss Giggle (with a Song), Mrs. Fidget and Waiter
(with a Song). *Harlequin Negro* had, in the way of additional characters, Magician, Clodpole, Don Stridero, Don
Guzman, Old Man, Calias, Captain, Sailor and Jenny
(with a Song). The cast of *Harlequin Mariner* is swollen
by the Fairy of the Oak, a Beggar, Tinker, Lawyer, Baker,
Lover's Servant, Alderman, Mrs. Fiction, Country Girl,
and actors playing the Vices.

The Continental story is there in essence ; the leap is
established ; but the pantomime has already undergone
both an anglicisation and a vulgarisation. Soon the policeman will make his appearance, and add his clumsy knock-
about humour to the piece. The old ballet-like formailty
is gone, replaced by various spectacular and mechanical
devices. The whole of it was, however, still mimed. A
few songs were introduced but there was no dialogue at all.

Finding that these entertainments caught the public's
attention, the manager of the Royal extended the already
loose interpretation of the pantomime form, and applied it
to completely original stories. Three days after the end
of *Harlequin Mariner* there was advertised

" A Grand serious, petit comic Pantomine Ballet . . .
called MATERNAL ANXIETY, or the Miraculous
Escape."

This announcement was followed by a synopsis, which

makes interesting comparison with that of *Harlequin Mariner* :

Scene I :

The only Daughter of the Spanish Governor of an American Settlement, being for some Years privately married (without the Approbation of her Father, to a young Officer then employed in the Wars, and the Issues of her concealed Engagement, a young and beautious Boy, secreted, with uncommon Caution, in the House of her Father) is seriously intreated to accept as a Husband a young Gentleman chosen by her Parents, whose Addresses she endeavours to evade and at last openly rejects, in defiance of her Father's stern Authority. On the Governor's Departure, the Child is produced from the Secret Repository which his anxious Mother had invented with curious Care to preserve his Life, and conceal her own Situation. On an Alarm of Hasty Footsteps, the Child retires to the Magic Cabinet, which has hitherto eluded the Vigilant Curiosity of the enraged Governor, but, in careless Haste, neglects locking a Drawer, wherein certain Letters are deposited, which might lead to a Discovery of his Mother's Situation. By the mere Effect of Accident, the Signal is given which draws the inadvertent and artless Infant from his Place of Appointed Concealment. The frantic Governor discovers him to be the Son of his offending Daughter, and, dragging forth the helpless Victim, cruelly resolved to offer the unoffending Infant as a Sacrifice at the Shrine of his Mother's Disobedience. The cautious Ingenuity, anxious Affliction, and maternal Tenderness displayed in the Management of this interesting Scene, is truly natural, domestic and affecting.

Scene II :

A wild and winding romantic mountainous Prospect. The Habitation and Residence of an outlawed Banditti, or Party of disaffected Indians and Spaniards, who are discovered in sharing their Plunder, and boasting of their barbarous Exploits. When the Robbers retire to the Cave, the Servants of the implacable Governor, employed to assassinate the Child, enter with their little devoted Victim, whose Fate seems suspended till the Ruffians have agreed upon the Manner of his Death. The Providential Arrival and Humanity of the Captain of the Outlawry rescues the Child from the uplifted Weapon of the abandoned Hirelings, and the grateful Boy repays his Deliverer with all the endearing Tenderness of Infant Affection. The Robber introduces the Child to the Banditti, who receive him with Kindness and Attention, and he retires with them to their Cave.

Scene III :

The distracted and wandering Mother in Search of her lost infant, is attacked in the Wood by two of the straggling Banditti, and released from their Brutality, by their brave and generous Captain. In this trying Situation, she unexpectedly meets the Object of her Sorrow—her beloved Infant, whom the Captain, with much Feeling and Regret, suffers to depart with her. In the Instant of their joyful Congratulations, they are again surprised by the Governor and his Assassins, whose horrid purposes are defeated by the Child's Possession of the Means and Manner of giving the Signal for the Assemblage of the Robbers, who now rush on and protect the Lady and her Child, and pursue, with unabating Fury, the Governor and his Ruffians.

Scene IV, &c., &c.

The accidental Meeting of the Father with the Child. The Alarm of the scouting Indians—his gallant defence and manly Retreat—the Terror and Trepidation of the unoffending Infant—the Presence of Mind and Intrepidity of a Female Black Attendant—with the animating and joyful Reconciliation of all Parties, form the principal Ingredients of this ingenious and well-contrived Ballet, to which appropriate Scenery, new Music and correspondent Decorations are all accurately annexed."

This explains, perhaps, why it became traditional to issue a book of words with pantomimes throughout the nineteenth century. They are so full and detailed that the reaction of the modern reader is sheer wonder that anyone, having read the text, would trouble to go to see the performance. There is no doubt that part of the reason for the book was advertisement, and advertisement not only of the pantomime itself, but of local tradesmen and goods ; but another purpose for it was surely to inform the audience of what was going on. The action of the mime quoted immediately above is so complex that it would require great skill on the part of the performers, and a highly sympathetic and perceptive audience, for the plot to become intelligible. This particular plot is not a well-known traditional story, and indeed there are many examples of the mimic treatment of serious and original stories at this time.

In 1796 *A Grand Serious Ballet Pantomime, in Two Parts, called the Death of Captain Cook* was presented. In 1798, an old dramatic figure took on a new guise in *Harlequin Doctor Faustus*. In 1800, something on more conventional lines was produced—*Harlequin's Arrival, or the Witch and the Sylph*. This affords another example of early and elaborate setting :

" In the course of the Pantomime, will be introduced, among others, the following new Scenes, &c.,—a Windmill and Cornfield, that changes to a Gunboat at Sea—Perpetual Motion—Hall of Chivalry—Doctor's Shop—Patent Coffin Warehouse—a View of Birmingham from the Warwick Canal, New Street, and Birmingham Heath . . . the whole to conclude with a Grand Picturesque Scene representing the Garden of the Sylph, brilliantly illuminated."

After this, the most notable contribution to the history

Plate IV

*ALADDIN'S
CAVE*

of these early pantomimes is the printed copy of *The Magic
of British Liberty*, mentioned above, which was performed
in 1805. It was specially written for this theatre, and is of
much interest in itself, besides being the earliest full text
of a Theatre Royal pantomime that survives—the next is
half a century younger. The changes which it displays are
remarkable. It opens with a recitative passage, and continues as a dialogue, with songs. The humour is of th.
cheapest kind—tawdry fun at the expense of a Frenchma\
speaking broken English. The text was obviously written
by someone who knew nothing about the nation he set out
to ridicule, and the consistency of the dialogue is quite
remarkable. The tradition, which lasts for another hundred years, of showing some mythological or allegorical
scene in the opening of a pantomime, is maintained by a
view of " Pluto's Dominions :— "

A Sketch of the New National Pantomime
Performing at the Theatre Birmingham

THE MAGIC OF BRITISH LIBERTY

OR

THE DISGREGATION OF BONAPARTE

With the Opening, Recitative, Songs, Prosaic Dialogue, etc.,
written by Mr. Cherry.

The Music composed and compiled by Mr. Holmes.

The Pantomime invented, selected and arranged by
Mr. M'Cready.

97

A
SKETCH OF THE NEW NATIONAL PANTOMIME.

The Pantomime commences with a View of
PLUTO'S DOMINIONS.

MAGICIAN :

    This scene of horror suits my gloomy soul—
    Where precious mischief occupies the whole;
    Where each sad victim bears his lot of pain,
    In torments endless destin'd to remain !
    Here SYSIPHUS rolls his returning load,
    And vile PROMETH'US gnawing vultures goad !
    Soaring IXION suffers on his wheel
    And TANTALUS enduring tortures feel ;
    There the DAMIADES fruitless buckets fill,
    And each offender bears his share of ill !
    Amongst these GRIEFS, some PLEASURE I devise—
    Come forth my imps ; ye sons of Fate ARISE !
        (IMPS *enter from cells*—)

1ST IMP :

    Say, are we call'd from yon deep dismal cell,
    To view the torments of this nether hell ?

2ND IMP :

    Or, if your friendship, on some frolic bent
    Shou'd need our service,—speak thy great intent !

MAGICIAN :

    'Tis fairly said, and rightly you divine—
    An imp of EARTHLY mischief must be mine ;
    Call from the dark recess of Pluto's cave,
    Him, whose ambition wou'd the WORLD enslave !
    Jaffa's murd'rer, fair Italia's plunderer !
    The Swiss destroyer, the WOU'D-be thund'rer !
    Let him on earth appear—CONSUL there ;
    But doom'd the mocks of all mankind to bear !

CHORUS OF IMPS :

> Appear ! appear ! for fiends too mischievous below
> Lest e'en the schemes of HELL thou striv'st to
> overthrow !

(BONAPARTE *rises on a pedestal, salutes the Magician and his Imps and is carried off on the shoulders of Fiends— shouting—flashing of fire from their torches, etc., etc.*).

MAGICIAN :

> Soft, lest success his fiendlike schemes shou'd crown,
> I'll raise a sprite to Britain's Nation known ;
> Various as their climate's healthful weather,
> Thunder, hail, and sunshine altogether !
> A fall'n rainbow feeds yon issuing blaze,
> From whose camelion tints my sprite I'll raise ;
> And 'ere his course on earth he shall begin,
> I name the motley hero—HARLEQUIN.

(*Lively music,*—MAGICIAN *waves his wand and* HARLEQUIN *appears*).

(*Recitative—accompanied*)

> From chaos call'd, now speed thee hence ;
> On earth thy mad career commence !
> This sword propitious wield for me,
> (*gives a black sword*)

> Who, from the deep, hath set thee free ;
> Whilst this black weapon you retain,
> Your power o'er mortals must remain,
> Unless some spirit from above
> Shou'd turn thy thoughts to bliss and love !

(*The protecting* SPIRIT *addresses* HARLEQUIN *and drives off the* FIENDS).

SPIRIT :

Hence fiends of night, thy purpose here forgo !
Caitiffs avaunt, to howl in shades below !
Here spangl'd fancy gilds each shifting scene,
And modest humour lends her ray serene !
A beauteous fair-one shall thy heart assail,
And many efforts in her cause shall fail ;
Thy chiefest foe t'whome bending nations crouch,
Shall be reduced to humble SCARAMOUCH.
Get hence ! Thy sable weapon now resign,
And frolic wield this magic bat of mine
                                    (*gives the sword*)
As thro' the wild fantastic maze you go,
Th' harmonic strain shall chase th' tripping toe.

   (*Song*—MISS BOOTH).

SCENE—THE GATES OF CALAIS.

(*A lively French strain played in the Orchestra*).

BILL BREEZE—*an English sailor, and* PATT BOWLING—*an Irish sailor enter cautiously.*

PATT :

O, by the powers of Saint Patrick, here we are, sure enough !—up to their very gates—the gates of Calais !—push on—push on ! and let us have a squint at their fortress.

(*Another French tune is heard while they reconnoitre cautiously*).

BILL :

Avast !—look to your bearings !—Do you perceive yon gun-powder scare-crow, resting his lank back against the gunnel of yon bastion—as if he supported the tottering building from falling on his head ?

PATT :

Shall I act a part of old parent Sampson, catch him by the heels—lug away the prop—and pull an ould house about his lugs ?

BILL :

Slacken sail !—damme, if you have a mind for a Sampson-rig, here's a better opportunity, we'll slay yon Philistine, and run away with the gates of the town !

PATT :

The Devil burn the failers ! and when the gates are open, we can send in an army of frogs from their own marshes, and make it a family quarrel, and put them all to death by the hands of their own relations !

BILL :

Shiver my Timbers !—is the peace and commerce of old England to be disturbed or prevented by the chattering of monkies, whose boasted success proceedes from having ravaged unoffending nations, stretching the grappling irons of their power to capture unprotected property ; marching uncontroul'd through countries, where, for ages, a musquet has never been shoulder'd, or a canon heard to roar ? Do the cowardly Swabs call THAT Courage ?

PATT :

Yes, honey,—French courage—THEY call it courage to catch a weazle asleep, or take a dead crocodile by the throttle :—the devil burn such courage as that, I say !

BILL :

And so say I, Brother Patt,—The timbers of a British heart creak at the bare mention of such unmanly boarding, damme, an Englishman loves to meet his enemy arm'd and prepared—sword in hand—face to face—and by a valorous display of strength and courage, support his KING, his COUNTRY and CONSTITUTION.

(*Here the* NATIONAL TUNE *played by the Band*).

PATT :

And to be sure. John Bull hasn't a nate backhand in his Brother PADDY ! And when SAWNEY steps in with his Andrew Ferrara, to assist ould Shilaly, the THREE UNITED ISLANDERS may sheet their enemies' beds with a shovel—or send them all to sup in ould Davy Jone's back parlour.

BILL :

Then—RULE BRITANNIA !
(RULE BRITANNIA *played in the Orchestra*).
(*Enter a* FRENCH CENTINAL—*frighten'd and yawning, as if just awaken'd from sleep*).

FRENCHMAN :

Ah !—Mon dieu !—sacre bleau !—vat is de matter ?— Vat is all dis musique and uproar ? It fright a-me from my post !

PATT :

I believe, honey, the tune was RULE BRITANNIA, and that is musick that has frightened your countrymen upon this very shore ever since the days of ould Edward the third !

FRENCHMAN :

Ah, ha ! Monsieur Jean Englis, for vy you have de bon audacité to venture on French land ?—Do you no fright. —Do you no fear ?

BILL :

Yes, as an English seventy-four does a French cock-boat !—as an emblem of my fears, I have just step'd ashore to see how the land lies, for, with a handful of my trusty countrymen, I have just now cut two frigates out of your harbour !

FRENCHMAN :

Sacre bleu !—'ave you no see de gran Proclamation ?

BILL :

No Monsieur ; but we'll overhaul your Log-Book presently ; and to convince you that an English seaman doesn't care a rope's end for French palaver, I have just step'd in to read it myself against the gates of Calais.

FRENCHMAN :

Den by gar you never step out again ! Ah, ha ! Vere is my weapon ?   (*Going to draw his sword*).

PATT :

Don't draw your sword honey,—or, if you do, I'll horse-whip you with the scabbard and thrust the blade down your ugly throttle !

BILL :

Ay—namme ! and stow the hilt after it, to prevent it from rising on his stomach !

FRENCHMAN :

O je demande pardon, Monsieur John Englis !—vere is your politesse ?—vere 'ave you learn your manners ?

BILL :

On board an English man of war !—Brave NELSON was my tutor, he taught me the manners of a British Seaman ; I finish'd my learning with him at the Nile, where he taught Frenchmen an English rigadoon, and made them cut mast-high capers to the tune of BRITONS STRIKE HOME!

(*The Band plays* BRITONS STRIKE HOME).

PATT :

There's a dancing maister for you !—I suppose Monsieur some of YOUR relations were at the Ball ?

FRENCHMAN :

No—begar de ball was at DEM.

PATT :

You are right honey—it was a forc'd meat ball—and like a good cook he serv'd it up with a hash of French calves-head.

FRENCHMAN :

Ah, ha ! morbleau !—our calf-head vill very soon visit your Spit-head, vat you say den ?

BILL :

Why, then we'll clap the heads together and, as we have often done before, blow you off the water, or tow every frog of you in Portsmouth harbour !

(*Music plays* HEARTS OF OAK).

FRENCHMAN :

Sacre !—vat you mean by frog ?

BILL :

Why, a sort of amphibious reptile ; a kind of Chief Consul of the ditches who, because he can dictate laws to lesser animals, presumes to proscribe English Freedom and even crush it in its grand palladium the LIBERTY OF IT'S PRESS !

PATT :

For which you see the PRESS-GANG is in arms—and if ever you shew your dirty whiskers at t'other side of the water, we'll bate you as black as a Dublin Journal.

FRENCHMAN

Oui ! You make a your brag vera well,—you 'ave take von, two, tree, little fish boats ah, ha !

BILL :

Yes, mounsieur, we have caught the French gudgeons.

PATT :

Yes,—and pickled the FLAT-FISH.

FRENCHMAN :

Oui—but we have de PIKE.

BILL : Yes,—but English seamen are SWORD-FISH—and damme, we'll give you SALT-EEL for your supper.

PATT :

And then you may PIKE it as soon as you please, honey.

FRENCHMAN :

Diable !—can Frenchmen bear von gran affronte ?—vere is your veapon ? Begar mine is out of my scabbard ! (*Draws his sword—the English sailor rushes on him, takes the Frenchman's sword and throws it from him, disdaining to use a weapon against an unarmed enemy*).

(*During the scuffle, the band plays—" O the Roast Beef of Old England "*).

PATT :

O, you dirty devil ! Wou'd you draw your sword upon a naked man ?—Is that your manners, and be damn'd to you ?

(*Lifts his arm to strike the Frenchman, which the English sailor prevents*).

BILL :

Avast ! Never let it be said that two British Bull-dogs worried a monkey !

PATT :

That's right, boy—(*to the Frenchman*). You see I have nothing in my hand but my five fingures ; but while I have a brogue with a foot in it, I can't help raising it on such an occasion. (*Kicks him*). There now—there is an Irish salute for you !

FRENCHMAN :

O diable ! Mon disgrace ! (*In a great passion*). John Englis, you be von scoundrel—villain !

BILL :

Blow me ! Here's a broadside. I'll run foul of your bread-room, and shiver your round-top like an over-bak'd biscuit. (*Knocks him down*).

FRENCHMAN :

O quartier !—diable !—am I to be murder ?

BILL :

(*Standing over him in an attitude—as waiting for him to rise*). No,—your flag is struck ? And a British seaman was never yet known to lift his arm against a fallen enemy. Bear a hand, Patt, and help him up.
(*They help him*).

FRENCHMAN :

Bear-a-de-hand !—begar, I have bear-a-de-FOOT.

PATT :

So you have, honey ; and now you are on your LEGS again, take to your HEELS as fast as you can scamper. If you ever forget how to run, devil burn me, but we'll soon larn you.

FRENCHMAN :

O sacre,—I vill be so revenge ! Vere is my veapon— vere is my sword ?

BILL :

Your sword !—damme, you had better cut and run !

PATT :

SHUFFLE off honey,—we'll cut for you at any time. (*Exit* FRENCHMAN). Is it CUTTING the poor devil is talking of ? Devil burn me but we'll slice you and bake you into the bargain. Ogh, I wish I had your maister, LITTLE BONEY'S whole army in an English oven ; with a gunpowder crust rais'd over them, they'd make a pie for the Devil.
(*Exit* PATT).

BILL :

Well, said Patt, ha, ha, ha !—Ay, ay, let Monsieur Frenchman brag and threaten—while Britons remember their hardy progenitors, he must be a daring enemy who presumes to venture on our NATIVE COAST ;— United in one common mass—The Attempt is SLAUGHTER, the Event is DEATH.
(*Song*).
(*When the Vaunting Corsican presumes to point out to his follower on " the road to England," BRITANNIA unexpectedly appears to him and speaks*).

BRITANNIA :

Hence, thou dark agent of foul Gallia's power !
On thy black deeds the frowning heaven's lour ;
Haste to the abode that fiends prepare for thee,
For Britons ever will be great and free !
This spear of magic freedom that I wield,
Is England's bulwark—her protecting shield ;
Nor racks, nor chains, nor slav'ry can impart
One ray of terror to a British heart ;
Thy reign is short—nor mercy canst thou find,
Thou pestilential scourge of all mankind.
Hence, phantom France ! and let the Tyrant see,
The seat of Arts and REAL Liberty.

(*Here* BRITANNIA *waves her spear* AND THE GATES OF
CALAIS *change to a view of the* BRITISH METROPOLIS.
Then follow the METAMORPHOSIS OF BONAPARTE *and the
various whimsical distresses that befal this doughty hero—
wherein many mechanical changes and entertaining transformation are exhibited*).

(*After the total Downfall and Disgrace of Citizen
Bonaparte*, BRITANNIA, *in the* TEMPLE OF LIBERTY,
thus addresses her people).

The Tyrant vanish'd at our dread command,
And confidence and peace possess the land—
Here Art and Commerce, with auspicious reign,
Shall breathe sweet influence on the happy plain ;
While o'er the lawn, with dance and festive song,
Young Pleasure leads the jocund hours along—
While shame and vengeance on our Foes are hurl'd
Shall ENGLAND reign the MISTRESS of the
                                        WORLD.

(*Final and general chorus*).

This, then, was the Harlequinade. Here can be seen the cleavage between the Opening and the rest. The text of the pantomime is, in fact, that of an extended, spoken Opening, on a popular theme, to be followed by a series of humorous adventures in mime. It will be seen that this spoken part becomes longer and longer, until the Harlequinade is left out entirely, and pantomime loses its mimic qualities altogether.

Mr. Cherry's was a National Pantomime. In 1813 there was a local one :—

> " Harlequin in Birmingham . . . a View of the Royal Hotel, Partial View of the Hen and Chickens, Clown is shot from a Cannon, and remains fixed against the Wall of the Hotel. Exterior of the Theatre Royal. Playbill changes to a Sedan Chair, from which a Miniature Harlequin escapes, and takes his Flight entirely round the Theatre. The Piece concludes with a distant View of Birmingham."

This use of local scenery was a popular device in the provinces, and was introduced into ordinary drama, as well as pantomime.

The various forms of pantomime of which examples have now been given, did not vary much until some time after the Christmas tradition was begun, by M. H. Simpson, in 1840. The first Christmas Pantomime is not strikingly different from its predecessors. It was specially written by De Hayes, and was entitled *Harlequin and the Knight of the Silver Shield*. It was full of dancing, scenic displays and effects, without dialogue. De Hayes was the author of the Christmas entertainments for some years afterwards, including two local ones, *Guy, Earl of Warwick* and *Lady Godiva and Peeping Tom of Coventry*. This last had a rhymed dialogue, of which fragments survive to show that it was a very cheap, humorous version of the old story.

The first extant printed copy of one of these pantomimes, *The House that Jack Built*, was written for Christmas, 1859. It contains ten scenes before the Transformation and Harlequinade. Their dialogue is in crude couplets, lame to a graveyard state, but with something of the satirical ring of Pope in them here and there. They are interspersed with ballads and songs set to popular airs of the day. Allusion is wide, ranging from *Venice Preserv'd* to *The Builder's Strike*. Little attempt is made to preserve a dramatic illusion, and the basic plot of the Opening is a sentimental love story. Some of the humour is crude and improper, and the plot has several unpleasant features—an elderly suitor, an ugly wife, a Lord enamoured of a servant girl in his household. The male protagonist was a man's role but there was a humorous female character played by a male comedian.

The same crude humour is to be found in *The Sleeping Beauty* in 1861. The story is taken from Planché, and much altered to fit local events—it includes jibes at the Watch Committee. The crudity soon becomes cruelty. It is one of the least attractive features of the age—a racy, slangy wit which is completely callous, and which is to be found in its most pronounced form in the racing papers of the time and in the brutal farces. It is not pleasant to find it in *Puss in Boots*. The whole pantomime is in very poor taste—a dead man's will is delivered in the form of a comic song. The humour of the piece may be gauged from the list of characters, amongst whom is " Tim O'Whackfoltherolidifinishemoffo." The most annoying part of the dialogue is the punning ; the text is full of this form of humour, which persisted for another forty years. Thus :—

"............. I've a scheme
To make your woods, with game of all sorts teem.
.... sprinkle well the soil
Throughout the forest, with Macassar Oil.
Rowland, in his advertisement, declares
It most encourages the growth of *Hairs*."

(Italics were in the printed text ; all puns were so marked).

In the Harlequinade to this pantomime of 1862, the parts were played by special dancers instead of " transformed " characters from the Opening ; thus the final break is made between the two, and although the Opening is still the subsidiary part it is growing longer.

The next stage in the metamorphosis is the introduction of troupes of dancers into the first part. In 1863, the pantomime was *The Queen of Hearts :* it had a scene called " The Nymphs of the Grove." The episode was thus advertised :—

" For this Scene has been engaged Mlle. Mazoni, assisted by a numerous and talented Corps de Ballet. The Ballet for which entirely original Music has been composed by Mr. W. F. Humphries, and the various movements arranged and produced by Mr. J. Milvako, of the principal London Theatres.—The Perfume supplied by E. S. Rimmel."

A commercial taint is already noticeable. The names of local tradespeople had for some time appeared in the book of words. The puns of this piece are more fantastic. The following seem to be directed at Major Gem, a contemporary dandy, and the reputed introducer of Lawn

Tennis into England ; but they are so involved as to be doubtful :—

" . . . . Dear Colin,
   Of gems you are the *Brummel*.
" . . . . Nay, for then
   This *Gem'mun* would be only *Brummagem*."

This degradation of humour is a pitiful thing to witness : it is also enlightening.   Consider these fermentations of fantasy in the *Aladdin* of 1866 :—

" Oh dear, oh dear, I'm of my boy *bereaved*.
  I *bereave* my boy, and I have been deceived.
  I'm *b'reft* of *all sopport*, and he, I fear

  Through his *bass* conduct's found an early *bier*."

In this can be seen the red-nosed humour of a certain class of modern comedian.   This is an early form of that species of wit whose first convention is that all mentions of drink, or its effects, are, in themselves, laughable.   In this pantomime there is also the beginnings of another convention which persists to-day—that of the comedian who leans over the footlights and takes the audience, especially the junior part of it, into his confidence.

" There you are wrong.   You search in vain, I fear ;
  I'm sure we have no naughty children here."

This juvenile section of the audience was growing—and the situations of the pantomime are becoming more and more childish.

Every scene now had its dance and song.   The latter were often advertised as " in character."   This meant appropriate dress and, perhaps, a backcloth.

. The pantomime for 1869, *Blue Beard*, presents one interesting feature ; its puns are as strained as ever, and it has the cruel humour of a fairy tale, but it opens with

Plate V
THE
AUDITORIUM
1901

a scene of pure mime in the manner of the earlier play. *Blue Beard* had an historical origin ; his story is said to have been popularised in England as a satire on the uxorious habits of Henry VIII. Millward, who wrote this version, was more concerned with the exotic than the historic :—

" Enter Blue Beard's Nigger Minstrels, African Ostrich Cavalry, Amazons, Cymbal Dancers, Turkish Troops and Blue Beard on his Elephant."

Stage animals and monsters had long been the fashion in London pantomime ; Covent Garden had quite a reputation for its stage beasts in the early nineteenth century.

Millward uses contemporary interest to give his poor dialogue a fillip ; for instance, a number of foolish sallies are aimed at Salt Lake City, and its community. He is fond also of the play on the slang mispronunciation of words, and ridicule of cultured accents. In his *Fair One with the Golden Locks*, played in 1871, he uses this device :—

" Woe to the Fay, or *faymale* that defies
A Gentleman of my superior size."

In this text there is also a trick, popular in all the lighter drama of the Victorian era, which persists until quite late, but which may surprise the modern reader, viz., humorous allusion, often in the form of parody, to the great classics of the stage.

The prevalence of this practice indicates that the popular audience of a hundred years ago was better acquainted with Shakespeare, and one or two others, than is the same audience to-day. This is borne out by the heavy Shakespearean bills of popular visiting actors and actresses. A little before this book was written, a clever quip in the same manner was made in a Birmingham Theatre, a quip based on a passage in one of Shakespeare's best-known plays. It was quite clear that not twenty people in the auditorium caught the significance of the line at all ; but in the eighteen hundreds, this sort of thing was commonplace :—

" You, as a crow can personate the role."
" It is the *caws*, it is the *caws*, my soul ! "

Not very brilliant, of course, but there was a new life-stream coming into Pantomime humour at this time, and one in which the Theatre Royal authors proved particularly happy—daring topical jokes. For the first time, though in stage history by no means the last, the Chancellor of the Exchequer is the butt of some shrewd darts. The latest fashions of the town—this particular one is in drink—are satirised :—

" And our American refreshment bars
In drinks of all descriptions cut a dash,
From ' corpse-recoverers ' to ' brandy-smash.' "

As Millward grows older, his productions degenerate into mere vehicles for fantasies of dancing, spectacle and popular sentiments. In the first scene of one of his last productions there are the most open references to Chamberlain, John Bright and Disraeli.

" *Discord* : In Glasgow lately, as you know, Old Ben
Appeared as champion for the working men.

Sphynx : A bid for office. He don't care a pin
For working men, so don't be taken in."

There is an entire scene in this vein, airing grievances at Income Tax, poverty, adulterated milk, the Plimsoll Line, dear bread and other things quite extraneous to the plot. Scenes are elaborate but short. An episode on board a steamer lasts for twenty lines ; the song before the curtain becomes a mechanical necessity. This elaborate Opening is now so-called by traditional usage alone, for it far outweighs the Harlequinade, which is on such lines as :—

"   I.   The Bull Ring and St. Martin's Church
(restored).
Caledonian Trip.   Harlequin and Columbine.

II.   A Butcher's and Baker's.   Grand Mazourka.

III.   Country Public House and Post Office.   La Polketta.   Departure of the British Troops for the Coast of Africa.

IV.   Coomassie in Ushantee.   Overthrow of King Coffee by British Troops."

The restoration of the Church, which was really a re-building of the whole, took place in the previous year—1872.   The " Trip " was a tour of the Caledonian Market in the Bull Ring.   The love of the military drama which was so typical of the Theatre Royal audiences is shown in the last two episodes.

E. W. Green wrote *Sinbad* for the theatre in 1876, and used the form better than his predecessors.   He with-holds the vile pun, writes lines which nearly all scan, introduces a simple morality, much like that of the melo-drama, and makes his couplets bite :—

" Why, e'en in England, parents, I am told,
Discard love's feelings, and go in for gold."

Lines like this would be surprising in a modern panto-mime ; so would these, which come near to being poetry :—

" As pines for liberty the prison lark
Or hard-worked sempstress in her attic dark,
So have I pined. . . . "

Hood would have liked this.   It is cheap, but its note is significant of the feeling of the town.   The temper of the whole age, its longing for the exotic, the " mystic East," which appeared in the popularity of the Aspidistra, also had its effects on pantomime. So in *Sinbad* there are scenes of Constantinople and the Golden Horn. Other panoramic views are on romantic lines too—a Rocky Serpent's Glen, and a Waterfall.

Green continues the practice of allusion to the serious masterpieces of the stage—in fact he goes further into literature, and refers to Fox's *Book of Martyrs*—but also employs crude, makeshift humour, for his industrial groundlings :—

> " In order that I may with others vie,
> I'll change my teeth, and try my new glass eye."

The cruelty of the fairy tale, the coarse Victorian cruelty in jokes about " niggers " or elderly amorous women are here ; yet, in the same text, come bitter attacks on the cruelty of Board Schools, and—vaccination. Food costs are pathetic material :—

> " Food here is dear, as dear as England quite,
> Where Saveloys are sold so much a bite."

The same tone prevails in *The Forty Thieves*, 1877, in which there are important structural developments ; the scenes, in fact the entire entertainment, become longer. Unpleasant humour—about the Salvation Army for example—still goes hand in hand with lines like :

" Is it a crime to have an empty purse ? "

" A crime ! Society knows nothing worse ! "

With the extension of the pantomime came the longer season, and although it still had not reached its present inordinate length, there was some discontent. In April 1880, a critic wrote :—

> " Theatre-goers are revelling in their emancipation
> from the long pantomime season, and at both our

theatres the Managers are spiritedly catering for their patrons."

In the following year, the authorship of the Royal pantomimes was taken over by J. J. Blood. In conjunction with F. Hall he wrote a version of the story of the Queen of Hearts, which was produced at Christmas, 1883. The first scene is a parody of *Macbeth*. The incantation begins :

" ' Here's the cat's paw that gained the monkey's nuts.'
' And here's a tooth child in convulsions cuts.'
' A glass of spirits mixed by Wilfred Lawson— '
' Nose of the statue raised, at first, to Dawson.' "

The last line is a clever touch, for in 1880, a statue of the public figure, Dawson, was erected in Chamberlain Place. There was a protest about it—the nose was too long—it was nothing like the man—so the offending effigy was replaced. Propaganda is still unashamed :

" ' They have the Tories for the Caucus spare,
the criticism Liberals cannot bear.'
' Yes, put them in, and add, 'mongst other ills,
The code of " cram " the Board School child that kills.' "

When the inversions of this last line are sorted out, it shows an increasing concern with education. The subject of school régime is frequent at this time ; political interest is, of course, noticeable in Birmingham throughout the reign of Queen Victoria.

Blood introduces a novelty—prose. In the best style of the English dramatists, he puts it in the mouths of low characters—Chorus of Cooks. His Harlequinade is still more curtailed and modified ; the traditional actors and actions recede before a spectacular *Masque of the Marriage of Cupid and Psyche*. The music hall adds its contribution in the form of *The Original Americans* and *The Midget Entertainment*. The Italian original is now almost beyond recognition. Yet Blood goes further on the way to end the old manner, not only of the Harlequinade, but also of the Opening. In *Dick Whittington*, 1884, there is homely humour, there are clever songs about the rates and the price of gas, but there is hardly a pretence of unity. The traditional story hardly appears at all and dramatic illusion is deliberately shattered. The villain, Fitzwarren, who, significantly, spends all his time electioneering, says

> " . . . . and I shan't cease
>   To be the willin' willin' of this piece."

A kiss is discussed thus :—

> " *Alice :* ' You dare to try ' !
>   *Gid. :* ' It is not in the part . . .
>   Now don't give way to fright,
>   We have to play in this scene every night.' "

The appalling pun is back again : it provides one of the puzzles of pantomime.

How, for example, was this conveyed ?

> " *Alice :* ' Meat ' !
>   *Dick (aside) :* ' Shall I now once for all tempt fickle
>   fate ?—O ?
>   Do not, sweet des*pot*(*h*)*at*(*e*) O—cold
>   Potato ' " !

How many of the audience had a book of words, and how many of them could read ? Surely very few spectators followed the dialogue from the text ; but without a text, many of these puns must have been incomprehensible.

The disregard of ancient and modern is no less remarkable. In the manner of the late eighteenth century, there is a " Grand Procession of Knights, bearing the Arms of the various Towns of the Midlands, and Workmen with the Emblems of their Manufactures." With this pageantry is more spectacle. The Transformation, now only such in name, since the Harlequinade is not danced by characters in the Opening, has now become " A Grand Transformation Scene, Luna and Rosy Dawn, designed and painted by W. F. Robinson." The way in which the form was being exploited to express almost anything which might appeal to the Birmingham audience will be clearly seen in *Robinson Crusoe*, 1885, in which Mrs. Crusoe appears as a Certified School Mistress :—

> " *Dame :* ' A Board School Mistress ! What a lot to teach
> The young ideas to shoot—beyond their reach ;
> To pass examinations ere they toddle,
> And cram with knowledge every little noddle;
> Until so closely packed, their little brains
> Resemble crowded, cheap excursion trains.' "

It might be thought, after reading such an excerpt, that Blood had taken an old story simply as a cover for the voice of his own opinions, but what he has really done is to take the title of *Robinson Crusoe* and present, under it, a gallimaufrey of popular devices from the cheap stage of the time. Once more the inevitable cannibal isle appears—not at all like that in the original :—

> " Procession of Tribes. The Cavalry and Elephantry. Grand Ballet of Squaws. Arrival of a British Warship. Conquest of the Island by the English Army. Aesthetic Quadrille by Rosa Troupe. Patriotic Song and Chorus."

This Imperial display is not all ; in Scene XIII is shown " Mons. Trewey's Wonderful Shadowgraph." Defoe would be hard put to it to recognise his own child here. The only thing which retains something of its proper form is the Harlequinade.

Cinderella, a story of great antiquity, is the only panto-mime subject which has been a favourite with both the nineteenth and twentieth centuries. When Blood handles this tale, he produces something more palatable and a little more familiar to the modern pantomime-goer. The story is both cruder and crueller than the one seen to-day—Cinderella is a servant girl, undergoing familiarities at the hands of an aristocrat employer, but the basic features are much as those still presented. Local humour is introduced—there is a family of the " de Birminghams,"—but the humour is noticeably better. Possibly the story may have been very well-known, so that Blood could not take too many liberties with it, or possibly more children were expected to attend.

The music for this pantomime was specially composed. Previously songs had been set to popular tunes. Now the songs were advertised in the book of words and the audience was told where, and for how much, copies could be obtained. From the extent of this advertisement, it seems that some of the songs had a chance of becoming popular, but they are now scarce. A few sheets of manuscript music still remain which were used by the orchestra in accompanying actors but these are very facile in construction.

The end of *Cinderella* is another spectacle :—

" Grand Elizabethan Masque, and a Procession of Shakespeare's Plays. Introduction——Tableau—— Shakespeare, Queen Elizabeth, Lords, Ladies and Attendants. Hamlet, Romeo and Juliet, Lear, Julius Caesar, Antony and Cleopatra, the Merry Wives of Windsor, Much Ado about Nothing. Twelfth Night, the Taming of the Shrew, and the Two Gentlemen of Verona."

Each character representing a play came forward and quoted two lines to form an epilogue.

This rather more pleasing pantomime was followed by a

bitter one. In the winter of 1887, *Goody Two Shoes* was given. The whole play was impregnated with local matter—it hinges on a Queen Anne farthing. One had been picked up in the Bull Ring, and, from the text, it seems that the coin had been manufactured in Birmingham, which had always had a reputation for counterfeiting. The attempt to make pantomime songs popular has already been mentioned ; in this entertainment it was continued, with the result that some of the songs take on a fierce political tone. One of these is so bitter, and so foreign to the modern spirit of pantomime, that it is quoted here in full :—

" And we true sons of Brummagem,
                    and towns that make the name
Of ' Black Country ' world famous,
                    starve for just the same old game.
The foreigner is in our midst,
                    with hardware right and left,
While English hands stand idle,
                    of their rightful work bereft ;
And markets glutted with the cheap
                    and nasty foreign trash.
Leave workmen going wageless,
                    with their masters gone to smash ;
While railways favour foreigners,
                    by granting them low rates,
And Free Trade (all one-sided though),
                    betrays us at our gates."

In the same pantomime there is a speech made up entirely of Shakespearean quotations, and the Harlequinade is expanded by the introduction of a new character—the Masher.

In the following year, the songs have become more specialised than ever. They are no longer composed by a local musician, but are selected from London performances, and sung " by permission of ———." They are composed

in a vulgar, music-hall style, full of strange choruses—
" Squeeze 'em, teaze 'em ! " the audience is exhorted. The
foreign is sought after as before, only now it seems that the
French may be tolerated again, *viz.*, " Scene Ten ; the
Eiffel Tower, and Paris Exhibition. Grand Ballet of
all Nations." The Transformation takes place in Titania's
Bower, " after a Midsummer Night's Dream."

The Eiffel Tower is preceded by a scene in a Pullman,
and followed by one in a Palace, but through them all
stalks a villain who cannot pronounce his " r's," except
when Blood makes a slip in the dialogue. The title of the
pantomime is *Alladin* [*sic.*] This illustrates the point
made earlier that the Extravaganza had a great influence
on pantomime. In Extravaganza anything might happen,
there was no touchstone of reality or probability.
Cinderella was followed by a Harlequinade of fairly conventional character but now shrunk to a tiny appendage
of the elaborate Opening.

The final decade of the century began with *The Forty
Thieves*. The story had been completely altered to fit a
popular theme of the time—the ruined family. This had
been used in the *Dick Whittington* of 1884, where one scene
was described as " Fitzwarren's Home, after the Crash " ;
the idea had potentialities at once comic and pathetic.

In this there is no greater attempt at a correct
geographical setting than in *Aladdin*. Indeed, the local
colour is laid on deliberately, and topical humour sought
after. Two characters who are still known in pantomime
were introduced into the Opening—the comic detective
and policeman—but the latter had had a part in the
Harlequinades at the Theatre Royal since 1876. Music
hall influence increased—several scenes were finished by

comedians and entertainers—and one concluded with a display of tandem riding.

In 1891, the authorship was taken over by Geoffrey Thorn. In his first venture, the story of Sinbad, he has an allegoric first scene called " The Home of Father Time " which is a revival of a regular practice. The villain of the piece, Rimbad, makes a formal declaration of his evil intentions to the audience in a manner clearly intended to ridicule the methods of the Melodrama. *The Bells* receives some shrewd comment and the stock phrases of the cheap stage—" Unhand me ! " " Die, villain ! " and the like are held up to derision. This may indicate a growing critical appreciation in the audience ; the text is certainly better than any for a generation, at least so far as diction is concerned. One character has a turn of speech that is akin to Falstaff's :—" Come forth, vile snip ! Bloated Button-stitcher, die ! " Yet structurally the work is just another hotch-potch. Into the middle of the wedding of Sinbad and Haidee comes " A Grand Procession, illustrating the Sports and Pastimes of England.' The Transformation represents the Seasons. The song with the nonsense refrain has reached the limits of absurdity. Audiences joined in singing " Lum tum diddiddley um di doo dah day." The debt to the music hall now included " Tararaboomdeay—the great London Success."

The decadence of moral standards in the entertainment world at the end of the century did not seriously affect the pantomime : it was felt strongly in the music hall, but the influence does not seem to have been passed on. The reason may be that more children were going to pantomimes. Humour is sometimes broad : in *Little Red Riding Hood*, which was written by Fred Locke for the winter of 1893,

there are some unpleasant jokes—quips on the word " tart "
for example, and much cuddling and " mashing " as it
was nicely called. A Children's Ballet, a comic donkey,
jokes about Gladstone, the Local Veto Bill, and Warner,
mingle grotesquely with such attempts at poetry as Red
Riding Hood's speech beginning :—

> " To granny's cot my way I daily take,
> While woodland choristers the echoes wake."

The final procession had now become a problem—
novelty was more difficult to secure ; but it was achieved
on this occasion by a " Grand Procession of Old China,
representing Old Chelsea, Coalport, Wedgwood, Dresden
and Crown Derby, followed by Grand Willow Plate
Ballet." The pantomime has a " Grand Medley Finale,"
and the Transformation is a separate spectacle ; it was not
followed by a proper Harlequinade—the last had been in
Cinderella in 1892.

The end has a touch of realism. *The Babes in the Wood*
for 1899, was written by professionals and not a local man.
One of the babes was George Robey. The script was
partly in prose, and showed an attempt at something which
had long been lost in pantomime—dramatic illusion. The
last relic of the old form—the Transformation—was left
out and there was no Harlequinade.

In 1900, *Dick Whittington* was making about £1,478 per
week at the best part of the season, which indicates the
growing popularity of the form. In 1902, the manager,
Mrs. Dornton, remarked that the pantomime had formerly
been only a part of an evening's entertainment, but was
now grown to an elaborate creation, requiring months of
preparatory work.

The new building began its pantomime career with an
elaborate *Babes in the Wood* in 1904, which lasted for four

and a half hours, and was a failure. Thereafter came a long run of successful pantomimes catering more and more for the juvenile part of the audience, and so developing a new style. The pantomime has now become a children's treat, and its season has grown longer and longer, encroaching sometimes on a fourth part of the year. Although little of it remains but the title to remind the audience of its early metamorphoses, it should perhaps be mentioned that revivals of some of the Victorian pantomines have taken place in London of recent years at the Players' Theatre, and that these have proved that the older forms have not entirely lost their attraction.

CHAPTER VII

THE LIBRARY AND REPERTOIRE OF THE
THEATRE ROYAL

THE collection of Theatre Royal play-bills in the Birmingham Library begins in 1790, and, except for the early years, is reasonably complete, but a detailed analysis of such an extensive set of records is beyond the scope of this book. The following remarks are based upon a summary of selected years which has been made from the larger collection. Details of performances before 1790 can be found in advertisements in Aris's *Birmingham Gazette*.

Ostensibly the character of these early programmes is musical, since the Theatre was unlicensed, but in fact the basis of all performances, from the opening in 1774 to the end of the first decade of the nineteenth century, was a play by an author of historical repute. Sheridan, Otway, Dryden, Cibber, and, above all, Shakespeare, were the playwrights whose works formed the principal entertainment of an evening at Birmingham's Theatre. The older dramatist was often presented in a form either mutilated or unhappily augmented. *The Tempest*, which had been long a favourite in Birmingham, and often on the bills of the old King Street Theatre, was played in the version " As altered by Mr. Dryden and Sir William Davenant, from Shakespeare." *Romeo and Juliet* was advertised " with a solemn Dirge," though it does not seem to have been given in the distorted version with the happy ending. Some unknown hand improved upon Cibber too, presenting in 1796, *Win Her and Take Her*, from Cibber's *Double Gallant*. The same year saw *The Follies of a Day*, which was taken, that is to say, stolen, from *The Marriage of Figaro*.

The first bill in the collection in Birmingham Reference Library is for July 21st, 1790. The main play was *The Jealous Wife* to which was added *The Musical Entertainment of Florizel and Perdita*. This is another example of the rough handling which Shakespeare received; episodes, in this case, one from *The Winter's Tale*, were taken and dressed out in fantastic trappings to form a convenient short " afterpiece." *The Sheep-shearing Feast*, from the same play, and the story of Beatrice and Benedict also appeared in a degraded and detached form, enjoying, to judge from their frequent appearance, some popularity.

In the main, however, a serious drama finds its way into most programmes of the time, even though it might be swollen with extraneous exhibitions of music and dancing. Much of this adulteration may have been made necessary by the theatrical licensing regulations, and the taste remained in the following century after the circumstances which caused it had passed. The tone of these early days is not altogether of levity, however ; there is even a slight preference for tragedy, and serious history. The favourites of the late eighteenth century audiences were *Hamlet, Othello, Macbeth, Lear, Romeo and Juliet, Richard III*, and *Venice Preserv'd*. On a lighter level, *The Tempest*, and *The Merchant of Venice* were best liked. *Much Ado About Nothing, The School for Scandal, The Beggar's Opera* and *The Conscious Lovers* were also shown ; but the taste of the audience may be judged by the fact that it preferred Sheridan's *Pizarro* to his comedies.

From these facts it must not be supposed that only plays by authors still recognised were popular at this time. Many serious dramas were then liked, and played repeatedly, which are quite unknown to the theatre-going world to-day. Among these the favourites were *The Earl of Essex* and *Jane Shore*, the latter remaining a regular success at the Theatre Royal for another century. It was played in 1792 " by particular request of the officers in the town." The bill advertised it " as performed for thirty Nights at Covent Garden, with universal Applause."

This remark is an introduction to one of the most disappointing truths about the provincial stage. In the eighteenth and nineteenth centuries, the country theatres were in the habit of showing plays which had had a successful run in London. Their repertoires show little attempt at originality. The stock company had a basic knowledge of the popular Shakespearean plays so that it could support the famous actors who came down from London ; for the rest, the manager was content to announce anything which could be billed as having recently run for thirty nights in the Metropolis. The Theatre Royal, however, had more originality than theatres in smaller towns, and local fare could be occasionally produced from a place of the size of Birmingham. For many years the pantomimes at least were all original. Moreover, several of the managers were playwrights in a small way, *e.g.*, Bunn and M'Cready.

When the early repertoire is considered, it should be remembered that the serious play was only the longest item on the bill—it was not the keystone of the evening on which all the other items depended. The programme was not built round the main play ; indeed, one of the most

entertaining and interesting features about these early
bills is the bizarre juxtapositions which they present.
When the Theatre opened in 1795, after re-building, the
main play on the first night was *The Earl of Essex*. This
was followed by a ballet, and the evening concluded with a
farce, called *My Grandmother*. A little later, *Richard III*
was rounded off by the same farce and a Scotch Dance. A
farce was the normal way of ending the evening, just as a
melodrama served as a tailpiece during Victoria's reign.
The melodrama, in the modern sense of the term, had not
come to the stage of the Royal yet, but a foretaste of it was
there. In 1792 was announced

" A Grand Pantomime, taken from the Ballad in the
celebrated Novel of The Monk, called Alonzo and
Imogen, or The Bridal Spectre."

It was in this wretched piece that the young Macready*
first saw Kean. In the following year, two other plays
which originated in the works of M. G. Lewis were presented—*Love and Cruelty*, which came from *The Monk*,
and *The Castle Spectre*. This early taste for a drama
which titillated the senses with the effect of horror, terror,
and nausea, is the beginning of the taste for something
stronger than the classical repertoire could provide, and
developes into the Victorian melodrama.

However, the fashion in drama was still reasonably good.
One reason for this was suggested by the historian, Hutton,
in 1781—" Perhaps there is no Period in which the Stage
is less polluted than the present, owing to the inimitable
Garrick."

Several major actors were concerned with the Theatre
Royal in its youth, and they must have had an effect on its

---

*Son of M'Cready.

programmes. Garrick, of course, did not play here, but
he did not die until the theatre had stood for seventeen
years. Since the provincial theatres sought so eagerly to
imitate the London stage, it follows that the great actor
would have had an indirect influence on Birmingham.
His *Miss in her Teens* was the afterpiece on the very first
night of the playhouse, 20th June, 1774. The first managers were themselves London actors. The Theatre was
built for the comedian Yates, who, except for a short interval
during which Miller of Shrewsbury was lessee, controlled
it from 1774 to 1792. Miller was in charge from 1779 to
1783, and the Theatre was closed for much of this time,
as the new portico was being added. Yates brought a
complete company with him from London, when the City
theatres closed for the summer. He was known as a
comedian, his wife was an actress of repute, and his troupe
was announced as " A Company of Their Majesties Comedians from the Theatre Royal in London," but the repertoire of this group was not exclusively comic. The year
of their reign to which the Theatre's historians usually
afford special praise is 1776 : in the course of it, Yates was
able to announce Henderson in the parts of King John,
Falstaff, Don Felix and Don John ; Mrs. Yates as Violante
and Constance ; Mrs. Young as Belvidera ; and Mrs.
Siddons as Mistress Ann Page.

Yates was succeeded by M'Cready, who began in the rebuilt theatre in 1795. He was not an actor of Yates's
calibre, and his talents were naturally eclipsed by those of
his famous son, though the latter was as yet unknown.
However, M'Cready was a spirited manager until the year
1808, from about which time the Theatre began to decline.
The reason throws further light on the high standards
of the early years. In 1808 M'Cready leased the Theatre

for the whole of the year, and set up as a purely provincial manager. Previously he had wintered in London, and had there selected his actors carefully. After settling in the country, he employed more and more strolling talent for small parts, and so gathered round him a large company of odd players. He had, of course, continued the practice of inviting famous players of the London stage to come to Birmingham and give a week of their favourite roles. Mrs. Siddons and the unstable tragedian G. F. Cooke came in 1801 ; Master Betty, the " Infant Roscius," in 1804 ; Grimaldi in 1808. In 1807, the Theatre had become Royal, so there were less restrictions on the nature of performances. Perhaps this induced M'Cready to take up full-time managership here in the following year. At all events, the state of the Theatre soon declined, so that, when his son made his stage debut in 1810, as Romeo, he was said to have " appeared to help his father, who was then in difficulties."

This account of early managers and actors may serve to show how strong was the influence of the Capital. There were, perhaps, two other reasons for the standards of the Theatre at that time.

First, Birmingham was then a fashionable town, with a core of families not aristocratic, but prosperous and of some standing. (This element has been dealt with more fully in Chapter Two).

Second, there was ever-present hostility from the Nonconformists. Bunn actually had sermons preached against him. A pamphlet war developed, in which many people seem to have joined. The results of the campaign survive, and their titles are of some interest.

These are as follows :—

"A Letter to J. A. James, with Notes, critical, religious and moral : by A. Bunn."

"A Letter to the Manager of the Theatre Royal, being a Review of his Epistle to the Rev. J. A. James."

"The Plagiary warned : a Vindication of the Drama, the Stage and Public Morals, from the Plagiarisms and Compilations of J. A. James, Minister of Carr's Lane Chapel."

"The Reprover Admonished, by a Churchman."

All these were printed in Birmingham during 1824, and the contest was known as "The Battle of Preachers and Players." Bunn, with malicious humour, put on a version of *The Hypocrite*, which packed the Theatre and caused the Rev. James some annoyance. Birmingham then had a strong centre of Methodism, and it may be that programmes were kept as reputable as possible in order to appease this element of the community, or at least not to annoy it too much.

It has been suggested that there was a decline from about 1808, but this, of course, was gradual. Elliston, who became manager in 1813, was at first only allowed to play three nights a week, because it was thought that there was not enough support for further performances. By the next season, the proprietors were congratulating him on his profits—£1,200. He had obtained these by re-sorting to popular, sensational tactics. Acrobats, equestrians, and professional weight-lifters make up many of Mr. Elliston's superbly worded bills. The rot had begun. Visitors usually gave a good programme : in 1815, Mr. and Mrs. Kemble gave a week of solid drama ; but this did not receive such advertisement as a pair of tight-rope artists, or the release of a cloud of balloons over the heads of the audience. Talent was still appreciated, however, for it was in this year that Kean took £263 at a benefit, thus defeating the record set up by Master Betty, who had made £232. Other notable players, such as Matthews, Payne and Conway came here : Elliston himself was an actor of some repute : but the equestrian drama was now firmly established—Birmingham audiences had been accustomed to it since Astley gave performances in the surrounding fields at the end of the eighteenth century. Now advertisements appeared outside the Theatre headed " Last Night but Four of the Covent Garden Horses."

Bunn, who succeeded Elliston, was not a very good performer, though his wife seems to have had a reputation for tragedy. They both acted quite often during 1820, but apart from Madame Vestris, whose first appearance on any provincial stage was made here in this year, the actors who visited were all nonentities. When the Theatre re-opened after the fire of 1820 the state of things seemed a little improved. The visitors made a fair collection of talent—Macready, Kemble, Ellen Tree, Farren, Power, Dowton and Elliston. The repertoire is significant. A play was shown in which may be seen the beginnings of the taste for a drama of humble life—

" *Martha Wills, the Servant Maid* . . . this Drama will be found to display a powerful, yet correct Picture of Humble Life, at once rejecting the Speculative and the Ideal . . . it will combine Characters and Scenes as they really exist in the World, casting a vivid and faithful Reflection on the Manners of that Portion of Society which it is intended, in the present Attempt, peculiarly to illustrate . . . Scene I—Nunky Gruel and his Victims."

Cheap sensations were provided by *The Iron Chest*, or, *The Mysterious Murder*. Performing dogs vied with military spectacles like *The Invasion of Russia*. One sign only is hopeful,—music came again to the Theatre. Two of the most famous virtuosi of the time, Paganini and Field, gave recitals, though their programmes were not of a very high standard. Byron's *Werner* was played without success but plays based upon the novels of Scott, domestic dramas and the Trial Scene from *The Merchant of Venice* were all popular.

Ten years show a lamentable change. In 1846, the manager could boast of elephants, horses and camels on his stage, but of scarcely a single good play throughout the year. Spectacle ruled, with domestic drama close to it. Edifying plays such as *The Anchor of Hope*, silenced the moralists. Opera was given by visiting companies, but they were rivalled by the tawdry burlesques, many of which were on the same themes. " Grand Romantic Dramas " were a commonplace of the bills. Pantomime was becoming highly elaborate, and the repertoire was profoundly affected by the craze for spectacle and variety. The cheapness of the time may be illustrated by an acrostic play bill for 1863—

> " The Pantomime concludes each Evening at eleven o'clock, allowing country Visitors sufficient time to return by the night train. . . . After the Farce will be produced a Talkative, Heartstirring, Enchanting, Attractive, Tremendous, Romantic, Effective, Rural, Original, Yearly, Ironical, Novel, Grand, Heroic, Annual, Magnificent, Comic Pantomime, entitled . . . &c."

During this year, the pathetic, moral, social and spectacular joined together in the production of *Uncle Tom's Cabin*.

The craving for the romantic and the exotic is very much in evidence at this time, taking the form of numerous plays with Oriental or Iberian backgrounds. Perhaps twice during the year, the Royal audience was shown how drama should be presented : Madam Mistori gave *Medea* with an Italian cast, and refused to have either curtain raiser or farce, and the Haymarket company gave a week of Goldsmith and Sheridan. The audience was unmoved : the favourite plays of the year were *The Trial of Effie Deans* from Scott, and *The Dead Guest*, which was more attractive than Scott, because it had Professor Pepper's Ghost in it.

There is little to be said about the repertoire from 1880 onwards ; all the major actors of the time appeared in those melodramatic roles with which their names have become associated. A list of the principal titles for the year 1897 may serve as an indication of what public taste was catered for :—*The Dancing Girl, A Bunch of Violets, Trilby, Hamlet, The Geisha, For the Crown, The Profligate, Charley's Aunt, Lord Tom Noddy, Royal Divorce, The Sorrows of Satan, School for Scandal, As You Like It, Twelfth Night, The Last Word.*

Chapter VIII

NINETEENTH CENTURY DRAMA

To conclude this study of the fortunes of one of England's largest early provincial theatres, a few comments are offered on the drama which it particularly well represents—the drama of the nineteenth century. The subject has already received thorough and distinguished attention, and a full account of it is not attempted here. Nevertheless, a few ideas about the dramatic literature of the last century have emerged from a study of one of its playhouses, and it may be worth while to have them outlined. Some will clearly be unoriginal ; some may owe their originality to the fact that they are based on the records of a particular theatre, and thus are not true in general, but since the history of the provincial stage and drama has yet to be written perhaps these remarks may contribute something to it.

The term " realism " will be used frequently hereafter, so we may as well begin by discussing its meaning. Dramatic realism is sometimes spoken of as though it were a modern phenomenon. As a term this is contradictory ; an audience is always obliged to accept certain conventions in stage presentation—it is, in fact, quite happy to accept them. These conventions vary with each age ; and one generation, smiling at those of its ancestors, is scarcely aware of its own. The citizen of to-day is prepared to enter a cinema and receive, as a representation of real life and events, a play of black and white shadows, and voices from an unseen source talking through the constant symphonic undercurrent of a muted orchestra. Yet many people claim that the cinema is " more natural " than the theatre.

So on our modern stage : as we take our seat at the theatre, we are quite prepared to see actions and to hear accents and speech which are not at all those of real life. Drama which was absolutely true to life—if such a thing can be even postulated—would draw no audience at all. That all art is artifice has been sufficiently laboured. " Realism " is a textbook term, and could probably be applied to some features of the dramatic presentation of any age. There is clear indication that the producers of the present are growing weary of it in its modern sense. Attempts are made to allow the spectators to share the life behind the scenes, which, it seems, creates a special familiarity with the actors, and a new sympathy towards their work. Scene-shifting is done quite openly, often by the performers themselves ; and the sets are commonly of a purely symbolic or functional kind. The symbolic variety favours a black back-cloth, or pillar, perhaps a surrealist décor ; for usefulness, a set of steps and a few chairs, with an upper balcony are simple and sufficient.

The use of contemporary dress for a play written in, or representing a former age is now commonplace ; and although it is sometimes used wrongly, to obtain a humorous effect, it is generally a sound device, and infinitely to be preferred to some of the costumes from the " period " property box.

The departure from historically accurate costuming is

greater than this. Now, a mixture of ancient and modern dress is sometimes used for certain effects. Thus the 1948 production of *Troilus and Cressida* at the Stratford Theatre showed some Greek soldiery dressed in duffle coats. The Birmingham Repertory Company, in the same year, draped their characters in oilskins during the storm scene in *Lear*. There was no effect of incongruity at all; the audience accepted what is the primary convention of all—that it was in a theatre. Symbolic costume is nothing new. It was used in medieval drama; it was used at the Theatre Royal a century ago, when the dress of heroes and heroines in tragedy had certain traditional details, whose origin is plainly symbolic : and it is used to-day.

In the nineteenth century, many of the conventions of the Elizabethan stage still survived, and it was, of course, much attracted to that period. The Restoration was too licentious for the Victorians, perhaps almost too satirical, for satire was not popular with our great grandparents. The Elizabethans, however, seen through the eyes of Mr. Bowdler, and so deprived of all bawdiness and cruelty, lived in a bold, bright, adventurous age. In one sense, the Victorian public had no roots, for a large proportion of it was the product of industrialisation. This created a society which had never existed before, and, because of its prudery and drabness, it had a romantic and sometimes unhealthy longing for colour and excitement. Hence arose the cult of the Gothic Revival, the raptures of Swinburne's Elizabethan criticisms, the numerous Shakespearean imitations of would-be serious dramatists and of established poets. We may smile at the opinions held about Shakespeare and his contemporaries ; but many of them are interesting, and in the same way not all

Victorians were fools. Macready played *Macbeth* in Birmingham, in 1841, and wrote :

> " I have improved Macbeth. The general tone of the character was lofty, manly, or, indeed, as it should be, heroic, that of one living to command. The whole view of the character was constantly in sight : the grief, the care, the doubt was not that of a weak person, but of a strong mind, and of a strong man . . . the novel effect, which I thought good, of restlessness, and an uneasy effort to appear unembarassed before Banquo, previous to the murder. The banquet was improved in its forced hilarity of tone ; the scene with the physicians very much so. It was one of the most successful performances I ever gave."

The romantic tendencies of the age also led to a sentimentality which is most noticeable in the death-bed scenes of the Victorian novel, and in the number of plays which ended round a dying man. Enoch Arden, for example, ends the play which bears his name thus :—

> I know that hymn, Doctor ! I have often sung it at my mother's knee—' O, come to the waters, ye who thirst.'—I come ! I thirst for the everlasting waters ! I come ! Annie ! Annie ! God for ever bl—(*Dies. Miriam, overcome, kneeling on one side of the chair, the Doctor standing on the other side, grasping Enoch's hand, and his head turned to one side. The hymn continuing softly till end. Slow curtain*)."

Those who have read *The Critic* may not be impressed by the pathos of the unfinished word ; but action is more eloquent. Thus in *Ravenscroft*, a favourite of the early days :—

> *They group round him. He beckons to Ravenscroft, and fixing his eyes on him, joins their hands slowly, then, turning to Alice, smiles, points upwards, and dies.*

There was thus an established kind of ending, grouped

round a dying figure, with tears falling copiously both on the stage and in the auditorium. Similarly, there was the bravado ending; the death of Robert Macaire is in this wise :—

> " 'Twas too late—yet it was a chance for life! I risked it bravely. Ha, ha, ha, ha! (*laughing wildly*) I have foiled you villains—I shall die like a man, and not by the hand of an executioner. Approach, young man : be kind to your poor mother, and pardon your guilty, inhuman father. (*Dies*)."

To return to the Elizabethan influence; several conventions of the nineteenth century drama seem to be derived from thence. Plays often open and close with a soliloquy, and the same device is frequent in the body of the text. It is quite ridiculous on a picture-frame stage, because it is a survival from a very different kind of building. A successful Victorian playwright claimed that the soliloquy was indispensable; it was certainly very useful, in the event of a fantastic plot and incomprehensible characters, as a device for explaining what was going on, and why. The soliloquy and aside are not objectionable in themselves, and it would be foolish to condemn them on the grounds that they are not realistic. In any case, the Victorian dramatist was not usually a realist; he might be a Member of the Dramatic Authors' Society, a country parson, or, like Planché, a Somerset Herald. He was prepared to construct a play with some pretensions to reality, which, in his clumsy hands, grew more and more involved, until it was necessary to unravel it by some fantastic device right at the end : the solution habitually lay in some facts suddenly brought to light, which had been unknown to both actors and spectators. In other words, the dramatist is using precisely those tricks with which Beaumont and

Fletcher titillated the jaded palates of the Blackfriars playgoers. The style has been satirised for all time in the suddenly-discovered relationships in *The Critic*, a play which the Victorians should have read more often.

Victorian soliloquies are too often displeasing because they are obviously utilitarian. The curtain rises to show an individual who, without being in an excited or emotional state, starts talking to himself. It soon becomes clear that he is there to tell the audience some details about himself and the plot. This necessity is a comment on the inadequacy of the playwright, and also a comment on his small knowledge of the theatre. The soliloquy, as has been mentioned before, was suited to an Elizabethan playhouse, with its apron stage, stools and intimacy. The Victorian theatre had no apron, practically no space before the proscenium arch, and a much larger auditorium. To convey a soliloquy, the actor had perforce to come up to the footlights and rant. This emphasised the artificial nature of the soliloquy itself, and may have encouraged the writing of them, as this style of delivery would provide a moment's glory to an actor with a bombastic style.

On the other hand, there is still a direct survival of what must be a very ancient custom of the acting profession—an address to the audience at the end of the last scene. In Colman's plays indeed, there is a formal epilogue, in the manner of the Restoration, but a more degenerate ending was usual, as in Brough's *Pretty Horse-Breaker* :—

" What do you think ? (*To audience*). Don't you think it's a good moral ? Say ' Yes.' (*To Bella*). Now then, after that you can have no objection to give me a kiss. (*He is seen struggling with her as the curtain falls*)."

There are many more examples of this trick in various guises ; for example, at the end of *Mother and Child are Both doing Well*, by Morton, the characters come forward one by one to explain and appeal to the audience.

Another sort of ending, which the Victorians evolved for themselves out of their own bad workmanship, was that contrived by a scene of pure action—usually a battle—in which all the tangles of the absurd plot were smoothed out, or cut. Thus :—

> *A Dagger drops beneath Caius's Robe . . . he falls dead. . . . Licinia throws herself on the Body. Cormelia, with difficulty, supports herself . . . the Consul and his Troops are heard approaching. She makes a violent Effort to recover self-possession, snatches Caius's Child from the Attendant, and holds it in one hand, while with the other, she points to Caius, confronts Opinius and the rest, who, immediately upon entering stop short. The Curtain drops. Flourish until the Curtain is quite down.*

Payne adopts this to the cheaper taste of the time in his *Ali Pacha* :—

> " *He fires his second pistol into a powder barrel, at the same moment that Ismail and the other two officers fire on him. The Citadel is blown up. Amid the confusion, and in a shower of fire, a general combat on the calcined rocks that surround the Citadel. Zenocles appears amid the flaming ruins with a banner.*"

This sort of device is understandable ; what presents more of a problem is not the silence but the speech. The diction of characters in a Victorian play is of two kinds only,—realistic speech for the low characters, artificial and sententious speech for the high. This was the standard usage of the Elizabethan playwright, with his alternate verse and prose, but the Victorians were not consciously imitating his practice, for its origin is in a truth of human behaviour—there is one standard of speech for the rich, another for the poor. The widening of education has by no means ended this distinction to-day, and it would have been strongly marked in that class-conscious age. No-one ever spoke like Othello, or quite in the idiom of Falstaff; but each represents the speech, imaginatively coloured, of a known type of man. Perhaps no conversation has ever been quite as brilliant as that in Congreve's plays, but he is never blamed for lack of realism. Yet on this score, artificiality of speech, the Victorians are condemned and ridiculed.

The following passage is from *Such Things Are*, by Mrs. Inchbald :—

" There are virtues which praise cannot taint—such are Mr. Haswell's—for they are offspring of a mind superior even to the love of fame. Neither can he, through envy, suffer by applause ; for his character is too sacred to incite jealousy, and conciliates the love, the respect, and the admiration of all mankind.

One's reaction to this is to say that it reads like a Victorian book of polite speech, or a Complete Letter Writer, though it was written many years before Victoria came to the throne : but the reaction is significant. It sounds like a certain period ; it has the ring of a particular time about it. The speech of Dickens' characters shows that, whilst his midwives and burglars speak in a manner which the reader accepts as real, allowing for the author's method of emphasising the grotesque, his educated or aristocratic young men use a diction which seems absurd and artificial. Yet this was not because Dickens did not know how such people spoke in real life, for, from his youth, he had often been in the presence of people of good education and standing. The novels of Charlotte Brontë show how the little girls at Lowood School addressed one another. The columns of any reputable newspaper of the time, the letters, the sermons,—all have the same ring about them. It begins to appear that, false as this ring now sounds, it was accepted, and actually used, by the Victorians. The tradition of an emblazoned diction in poetry was still maintained by Lord Tennyson ; the courtly manners of the eighteenth century were retained for use, even in business ; perhaps some people still practised speech as a conscious art. Nor was the nineteenth century alone in pompousness. The writer recently had the opportunity of looking through a private collection of Warwickshire and Leicestershire epitaphs from which came the surprising truth that the memorial verses of the Victorians were much simpler than those of their grandfathers.

At all events, speech reproduced with absolute fidelity from real life is of no use to the dramatist ; people in time of great emotion, are apt to say trivial or banal things. This has been immortalised in a famous line from *Lear*, but there is only one Shakespeare.

Hardly anyone has tried to suggest that the drama of the time is of any value : many writers do not consider it seriously at all, those who do assume at once that it is of poor quality, and try to explain why. It would be rash and impractical to propound here any thesis that all these critics are mistaken ; but an examination of some of the factors with which the playwright had to contend may at least help to dispel that attitude of contemptuous mockery which is so often taken towards the period.

A debate in the House of Commons in 1832 decided that the drama was declining (it was something of which everyone was perfectly well aware) because of legal restrictions, the small size and resources of many of the theatres, and the commercial outlook of the managers. All these have been seen to affect the Theatre Royal, except the size of the house. The influence of commercial interests on all forms of art is a subject worthy of study, from aristocratic patronage to box office returns. The last ten years have seen a flood of films, of a steadily declining standard, about the war. At the time of writing, several films of the very worst kind, based, it is untruthfully claimed, on the lives of various famous musicians and authors, are being shown in this country. These forms of film have been evolved, and their possibilities exploited to the point of artistic ruin, because they have had an initial commercial success. No doubt the Victorian manager put on the plays which his audience wanted.

It has been claimed that the Victorian Age had a general disposition to expansiveness, as exemplified by the long poem, the novel, the architecture, the furniture. This has been blamed for the failure of the drama. It may perhaps have been a contributory cause towards the undramatic qualities of the poetic drama, though the reasons for the expansiveness of Swinburne and Browning were not such as would affect the age in the mass. The answer to the whole question of the drama seems rather to lie with a part of the theatre which is the least to be considered by the academician, the first by the playwright—the audience. The new teeming industrial city produced an audience which wanted cheap, easily-assimilated amusement. It is often said that an Elizabethan audience was a representative one ; but it is hard to imagine that there were then many workmen who could lay down their tools at noon, and spend the rest of the day in the theatre. Workmen and apprentices were under a hard discipline, and continued to be, as the eighteenth century newspaper warnings against harbouring runaways testify.

Cruikshank's cartoon, *Pit, Boxes and Gallery*, shows roughs in the Gods, a Pit full of tradespeople and clerks, and Boxes occupied by an unæsthetic and rakish section of the upper classes. This audience was not one which went to a play because the Press gave it a good criticism—there were few critics who knew what they were talking about, and the incidence of illiteracy was very high.

> " They come jaded from the impure air of shops, factories and offices, from the hard stress of professional or domestic duties, and they are incapable or impatient of the intellectual exertion and prolonged attention necessary to judge a serious work of art . . . the great majority of playgoers never have come to the theatre for literature and poetry, for any kind of moral, artistic or intellectual stimulus, or for any other purpose than mere amusement or pastime." (H. A. Jones. *The Renascence of the English Drama.* P. 247).

" Never have come." Did the Elizabethans go to the play for moral instruction? They wrote plays with a moral basis, because, as Sidney assures us, that was the purpose of drama : but they were careful to stuff their plays with dumb-show, fooling, pageantry, bawdry, songs for the ladies, pun-play for the wits, sensuous verse for the exuberant. The greatness of the Elizabethan author lies in his good use of those things which the audience required of him. Like the medieval artist, painting his patrons into a religious picture, he applied his art ; and with wonderful results. When, as happens a little later on, the audience is of a uniform kind, a particular genre develops ; thus the plays of the Restoration are all in the same key. The audience widens again, drama goes into the country, where the standards would be lower than in London, and the fare becomes mixed once more. As the nineteenth century develops, the heterogeneous appendages grow to a life of their own, and the moral and artistic core which is necessary to all good drama grows weaker and weaker. Thus in the melodrama, sensationalism, which popular audiences have always loved, has developed out of all proportion, but the morality survives in the usual triumph of virtue over villainy.

Perhaps one of the reasons for the failure of the Shakespearean imitations was that the writers sought only to imitate his noble parts, and, in the interests of taste and morality, avoided those things imposed upon him by his audiences, and so effectively used. An expurgated Shakespeare is a poor thing. His plays in his own time probably had short runs, and then revivals ; the Victorians generally had short runs, and, having exhausted the novelty of the play, saw no revival. The dramatist turned his plays out quickly—he had to :—

> " One line, one first night, that presents a view of life foreign to that which obtains in Tooley Street or Gotham, may so upset three wrathful gentlemen from Tooley Street or Gotham, who may chance to be in the house, that they may conceive themselves bound, by the sternest sense of duty, by all that they owe the drama, to themselves, to the public, and to Tooley Street or Gotham, to protest against the piece, and, so far as they can, to prevent its being heard, or heard of, again." (H. A. Jones, *Op.Cit.*).

So there had to be another play ready. The key word to the age is not expansiveness, but prolificacy. Because the Victorians built large gas-works and town halls, and wrote novels in three volumes, a sudden racial tendency to expansiveness is not to be deduced. The Elizabethans are not called diffuse ; but Spenser and Milton knew how to write a work as long as anything the Victorians could show.

Brevity is necessary to the drama, and until the advent of Shaw, Victorian drama is of standard length,—the one-act farce is more common than the three-act melodrama ; this again more than the five-act tragedy. Yet these short plays are diffuse within their own narrow bounds. The long play-bill was not an indication of a desire for length, but for variety. Its first cause was the half-price system :

> " We shall ever loudly condemn the practice, too much resorted to, of putting so much in a benefit bill, being quite sure that, after a certain hour (say 11 o'clock) the audience invariably get tired, and the actors invariably stupid."

This was in 1825, at Birmingham.

Individual popularity must have had as much to answer for, as it has in the present day entertainment world. Popularity is a capricious thing. The great archæological revivals were very popular, but for the wrong reasons. They do not indicate a real antiquarian interest at all, except, perhaps, on the part of men like Planché, who knew a little about the subject. They were simply the product of a cheap desire for display, and of that longing for the romantic, barbaric, Gothic, and—favourite word of the Victorian advertisement—*genuine* past which has already been discussed. The age was not a very healthy one. One regards with abhorrence the attitude of mind which is expressed by the common use of the phrase " Unfortunate Female," when it is seen in its true perspective—along with the Can-Can, the cheap, slangy humour of the sporting papers and garish music halls, the side-whiskered, cheroot-smoking Masher, and the play bills of Adah Menken. Late night-life, slums, tired women and cheap gin seem to play a large part in the Victorian symphony. In the theatrical world, the results were the plump pantomime artiste, and the distasteful farce, which, while its dialogue is strictly controlled, has nevertheless a basis which is often purely sexual. Such pieces—J. M. Morton provides many examples—are unpleasant in the extreme, full of innuendo and nasty allusion.

We are constantly coming back to the audience : but the whole blame may not be carried into the Gallery and left there. Somehow, the Victorians were lacking in original dramatic subjects. An enormous number of plays were billed " adapted from the French," and if all managers had been honest, a great many more would have been so announced. An adaptation simply meant a very free translation. The following two comments, made by men who knew the theatre well, are of value :—

> " A man all in black—a chattering steward—a young lady—a little child—and fire-works, are the constituents of two or three dozen French things that the English have been fool enough, in the past years, to import from that trumpery nation."

Waterloo was only ten years past when this was written ; so that the author may be forgiven for overlooking the fact that these constituents made up many an English play, too. The second excerpt is from a lecture at the other end of the century :

> " It is a fact, that the manager of our leading comedy theatre has produced only one original play of English authorship for the last eight years, and is now contemplating the revival of a French Adaptation."

Was this because the French drama, neater, salacious, was more attractive than the English ? Or was it because of the easy Gallic emotions ? Emotion was certainly favoured—so much is clear from the number of plays made from Dickens' novels, but this again illustrates the lack of dramatic material.

However, when a full length play, by a popular English author, and an emotional one too, was produced at the Theatre Royal, in 1827, it received the following official criticism in the Press, after its first night.

" Although this tragedy might please the cocknies (*sic*), it did not answer our expectations, in the first place it is too long and tedious, the plot is bad, we consider the piece would have greater interest if concluded one or two acts sooner, there is also much improbability about the piece, to say nothing of natural feeling and in our opinion not worth the loss of time in setting down."

The play was *The Two Foscari*. At least Lord Byron's punctuation was better.

The Theatre Royal has had nothing very remarkable in its history—two fires, but no other disasters : some famous actors, but only Macready with any strong connection : a fine building, but now replaced. Nevertheless, its story is one of interest, because it is linked with one of the great, expanding industrial towns of the nineteenth century, and because it reflects, in a faithful fashion, the trends of the provincial stage during a period whose drama is so seldom considered at all.

BIBLIOGRAPHY

Warwickshire, by Clive Holland.

History of Birmingham, by Hutton, 1809.

Survey of the Borough and Manor or Demesne Foreign of Birmingham, made in the first year of the reign of Queen Mary, 1553. Transcribed by W. B. Bickley, with notes by J. Hill.

Victoria County History, Warwickshire.

Showell's Dictionary of Birmingham, ed. T. T. Harman.

Britannia, by Camden, 1695.

Aris' *Birmingham Gazette.*

Street Directory for 1777, by C. E. Scarse, 1896.

The Making of Birmingham, by R. K. Dent.

The Theatric Tourist, by J. Winston.

On the Stage, by Dutton Cook.

A Century of Birmingham Life, by J. A. Langford.

A Short History of the Theatre Royal, by R. C. Rhodes.

Philip Rodway and a Tale of Two Theatres, by Rodway.

Early Victorian Drama by E. R. Reynolds.

Ellistonia, by Charles Lamb.

The Story of the Black Country, by F. W. Hackwood.

The Theatrical Looker On at the Birmingham Theatre.

Macready's Reminiscences, edited by Frederick Pollock. 2 vols., 1875.

The Drama of Yesterday, by Clement Scott.

Stage Effect, by Mayhew.

Lamb's " Barbara S— " by L. E. Holman.

The History of Costume on the English Stage, contained in
  Studies of Members of the Department of English, Uni-
  versity of Wisconsin, Series I.

Charles Dickens, by Una Pope-Hennessy, 1947.

Ye Old Theatre Royal, by T. E. Pemberton.

Christmas Pantomime, by A. E. Wilson.

A History of Pantomime, by R. J. Broadbent.

Clowns and Pantomimes, by M. W. Disher.

The Development of the Theatre, by Allardyce Nicoll.

The Renascence of the English Drama, by H. A. Jones.

Apology for Poetry, by Sir Philip Sidney.

Reference has also been made to many Birmingham
newspapers of all periods, to the Crompton Rhodes Collection, and to playbills, pantomimes, and unpublished
manuscripts (including the Minute Books of the Proprietors
of the Theatre Royal).

" Catalogue of the Superb Wardrobe, Theatrical Library, Music, Properties, Scenery, Deal Planks & Other Effects, which will be sold by Auction, by B. Chesshire, at the Theatre Royal, Birmingham, on Monday to Saturday, the 25—30 Days of April, 1825. The Sale to begin each Day at 10."

[The complete Catalogue is not reproduced here, only the list of scenery and the dramatic library].

Scenery : " Foreign Cottage, modern Gothic : Moonlight flats : modern Gothic wings : wall piece : pair of ancient Streets : two cut trees : Topax Chamber, with two doors : Loch Katrine, and two flats : Moonlight Glen : two large rock pieces : foreign landscapes and wings : Library : Saxon hall : pair of mountain flats : Gulph of Cambray : transparent wood : 1 pair of barn flats : transparent Diorama : fire piece (Revolt of the Greeks) 3 pieces of a Torrent : 2 pairs of Ship flats : transparent Horizon : view of Genoa : Midas' car : Willow Tree piece ; Tom and Gerry Scene piece : Cutler's shop : secret mine : 2 balustrade raking pieces : 2 columns (Revolt of the Greeks) Cave side piece : 2 cut wings : Cherry's Garden, setting piece : Alley side piece : 3 set pieces (Miller and his Men) Timon's breaking wall : rock piece : row of set pieces (Three Fingered Jack): 2 Indian huts : 2 pairs gates : 4 breaking pieces : 2 setting pieces (Maid Marian) Holyhead Lighthouse : Belfry setting piece : back of throne : 1 row rocky landscape : side piece to Belfry : 1 pair of doors : 1 raking balustrade : side piece with two doors : two gates :

Jack's cottage : burning cottage : two small trees : 2 raking pieces (Secret Mine) : Othello's bed : 1 odd wing : 2 Castle flats : Wellington, trees, 2 flats : Marchienne du Pont : English Bivouac : Village of Waterloo : Observatory : rainbow setting piece : cataract—2 rows, 2 setting pieces : moonlight scene : 2 Elephant wings : Timour's gate : Edgerow : 2 border battens : 2 large rock pieces : Thereses Pavilion : rock piece : Cherry's boat : Brutus' gate and walls : 2 landscapes : satin chamber : 2 palace flats and wings : 2 arch flats, 2 blue screens : rainbow : New Street, 2 flats : trick fire guard : Cross : Macbeth's cauldron : breaking tree : hot house complete : Der Freischutz, 13 pieces : rolling waters with barrels : Aloe : 3 long troughs : Kenilworth : bridge with ropes and pulleys : sinking piece— Cherry and Fair Star : wood beam and trap : battening rain and frame : pantomime trap : flying apparatus : rustic bridge : Cloud border : Gloriana car : 4 clouds : Cleopatra's Gallery and Truck : lion truck : peacock car : Vulcan's Forge : Columbus—3 breaking pieces : rack wheel, Harlingford Castle : canvass boat, 2 small balconies : drawbridge : Watch House bar : artillery carriage in Timour : tight rope : horizon cloth and shaking waters : Horse Timber."

The Dramatic Library :—" Alexander the Great, Alphonso, Amoroso, All for Love, Adrian and Orilla, Actress of all Work, Addlemen, The Antiquary, All in the Wrong, The Adopted Child, As You Like It, Arthur and Emily, Adeline, The Apostate.

The Battle of Hexham, Brutus, Belle Stratagem, Bankrupt, The Busy Body, The Beaux Stratagem, The Blue Devil, Beggars' Opera, The Brothers, The Bee Hive, The Blind Boy, Bellamira, Boarding House, A Bold Stroke for a Husband, The Birthday, Blue Beard, Bertram, Barbarossa, Blind Bargain.

Constant Couple, Confederacy, Cymbeline, Cent per Cent, Comus, Caius Gracchus, Castle of Andalusia, Chances, Coriolanus, Castle of Torento, Chip off the old Block, Chapter of Accidents, Counterfeits, Children in the wood, Castle Spectre, Cure for the Heart Ache, The Critic, Clandestine Marriage, Comedy of Errors, The Citizen, Clari, Conrad, Count of Narlonne, Catch Him Who Can, Cymon, Child of Nature, The Curfew, Cato, Conquest of Terunto.

The Duel, Damon and Pythias, The Duenna, Delays and Blunders, Distressed Mother, King John, The Deserted Daughter, The Dramatist, Douglas, The Double Dealer, De Mountford, Drummond, David Rizzio, The Delinquent.

Evadne, The Black Prince, Edgar and Emmeline, Every Man in his Humour, England Preserved, Earl of Warwick, Earl of Essex, Elfrida, Education, English Fleet, The English Merchant, Electra, Ella Rosenburg.

Fontainbleu, Folly as it Flies, The Follies of a Day, Falls of Clyde, Flitch of Bacon, The Farm House, The Fair Penitent, The Funeral, Frederick the Great, Faulkner, The Foundling of the Forest.

Guy Mannering, Guy Fawkes, The Gambler, George Brunwell, The Grecian Daughter, Goodnatured Man, The Gentle Shepherd, The Gamester, The Gazette, Guilty or Not Guilty? The Green Man.

The Hypocrite, Henri Quatre, Hamlet, The Honeymoon, Heir at Law, He would be a Soldier, The Haunted Tower, High Life Below Stairs, The Hero of the North, Henry VIII, Half Hour after Supper, The Humorous Lieutenant, Hear Both Sides, How to Die for Love, High

Notions, Helpless Animals, Hearts of Oak, High in the City.

Julius Cærsar, The Inconstant, I'll Tell You What, Irish Widow, The Innkeepers' Daughter, The Italian Monk, Inkle and Yarico, Incognito, Indiscretion, The Irish Tutor, The Irishman in London, Ivanhoe.

Joan of Arc, Julien, Jane Shore, The Jealous Wife, The Jew of Lubeck, Isabella, Know your own Mind, Richard II.

Killing No Murder, Knight of Snowdon, Catherine and Petruchio, Henry V, Kenilworth, Lady of the Lake, Lovers Quarrel, Love Laughs at Locksmiths, Lost and found, Lionel and Clarissa, Law of Java, Lodiska, Living in London, Life, The Libertine, Lovers' Vows, Love on a Village, The Lady and the Devil, The Merry Wives of Windsor, Macbeth, Maid of the Mill, Midnight Hours, Man of the World, Maid of Bristol, Marriage Promise, Midas, Magpie, Measure for Measure, The Mourning Bride, May Day, Maid or Wife, Marriage of Figaro, Medea.

Native Land, Nigel, No Song, No Supper, New Way to Pay Old Debts, The Old Bachelor, The Quadrille, The Poor Gentleman, Peter Fin, The Pannel [Sic], Plot Counter Plot, Past Ten O'clock, The Orphan, Oroonoko, The Peasant Boy, Pizarro, The Provok'd Husband, The Padlock, Othello.

Richard III, The Review, Raising the Wind, Riches, Rich and Poor, The Rivals, Royal Oak, Road to Ruin, Remorse, Rage, The Rendezvous, Roland for an Oliver, Ruhantino, Rob Roy.

Speed the Plough, She Stoops to Conquer, Such Things Are, Soldier's Daughter, School of Reform, She Would and She Would Not, The Stranger, School for Scandal, Sleep Walker, Sprigs of Laurel, Suspicious Husband, The Steward, The School for Fathers, The Spectre, Sappho,

Sons of Erin, The School for Authors, The Slave, Smiles and Tears, The Sleeping Draught, Students of Salamanca, A Short Reign and a Merry One, Speculation, A Sea Side Story.

Tom and Gerry, Turnpike Gate, Therese, Tom Thumb, Thomas and Sally, Trial by Jury, Two Gentlemen of Verona, The Travellers, Twelfth Night, Tamerlane, Turn Out, Town and Country, Tekeli, Too Many Cooks.

Virginius, Venice Preserv'd, Venetian Outlaw, Venoni, The Vampire, Virginia, The West Indian, The Way to Keep Him, Ways and Means, Wild Oats, Winter's Tale, Wallace and the Weathercock, Wives as They Were, The Warlok of the Glen, Where Shall I Dine ?, The Wanderer, Which is the Man, Wife with Two Husbands, The World, Who Wants a Guinea, The Woodman's Hut, The Way to get Married, The Wheel of Fortune, The Well.

King Lear, Youth, Love and Folly, Peeping Tom, The Son in Law, Dead Alive, The Spoiled Child, The Agreeable Surprise, Grandmother, No Song No Supper, Paul and Virginia, The Poor, The Twins, The Deserter, Commissary, Three Weeks After Marriage, Bon Ton, All the World's a Stage, Contrivances, Spirit of Contradiction, The Patron, Day After the Wedding, Bombastes and Ataxerxes, Darkness Visible, Is He Jealous, The Highland Reel, Zemluca, The Sultan and the Romp, Midas."

The order is as in the Catalogue : 55 other Dramatic Pieces were advertised ; as they were in manuscript, their names were not given.

ACKNOWLEDGMENTS

A full list of all those who, by advice, information, criticism and encouragement have helped the writer is not possible here. Certain debts, however, must, because of their outstanding nature, be acknowledged. To the following, then, sincere thanks are due :—

> Dorothy M. Norris, F.L.A.
> Barbara M. Garratt, B.A.
> Barbara Bowen, M.A.
> Robert J. Hetherington, Esq.
> Ernest R. Reynolds, Ph.D., B.A.
> Robert V. Rowland, B.A.

Several people have also responded very helpfully to begging letters from a total stranger, among them the late Maud Gill, Phyllis Bushell-Matthews, B.A., and the present Manager of the Theatre Royal.

黎庠圖書社
LIM M. LAI
PRIVATE LIBRARY